140 HOT & SPICY CHICKEN DISHES

140 HOT & SPICY
CHICKEN DISHES

A SIZZLING COLLECTION OF FIERY CHICKEN AND POULTRY
RECIPES WITH OVER 170 PHOTOGRAPHS **VALERIE FERGUSON**

southwater

This edition is published by Southwater, an imprint of Anness Publishing Ltd, Hermes House,
88–89 Blackfriars Road, London SE1 8HA; tel. 020 7401 2077; fax 020 7633 9499

www.southwaterbooks.com; www.annesspublishing.com

If you like the images in this book and would like to investigate using them for publishing, promotions or advertising,
please visit our website www.practicalpictures.com for more information.

UK distributor: Book Trade Services; tel. 0116 2759086; fax 0116 2759090; uksales@booktradeservices.com;
exportsales@booktradeservices.com
North American distributor: National Book Network; tel. 301 459 3366; fax 301 429 5746; www.nbnbooks.com
Australian distributor: Pan Macmillan Australia; tel. 1300 135 113; fax 1300 135 103; customer.service@macmillan.com.au
New Zealand distributor: David Bateman Ltd; tel. (09) 415 7664; fax (09) 415 8892

Publisher: Joanna Lorenz
Editorial Director: Helen Sudell
Consultant Editor: Valerie Ferguson
Recipes contributed by: Catherine Atkinson, Alex Barker, Angela Boggiano, Kathy Brown, Carla Capalbo, Lesley Chamberlain,
Kit Chan, Maxine Clarke, Frances Cleary, Carole Clements, Trish Davies, Roz Denny, Michelle Berriedale-Johnson,
Patrizia Diemling, Matthew Drennan, Sarah Edmonds, Joanna Farrow, Rafi Fernandez, Christine France, Silvana Franco,
Sarah Gates, Shirley Gill, Rosamund Grant, Carole Handslip, Rebekah Hassan, Deh-Ta Hsiung, Shehzad Husain,
Christine Ingram, Judy Jackson, Soheila Kimberley, Masaki Ko, Ruby Le Bois, Lesley Mackley, Norma MacMillan, Sue Maggs,
Kathy Man, Maggie Mayhew, Norma Miller, Sallie Morris, Elizabeth Lambert Ortiz, Maggie Pannell, Katherine Richmond,
Anne Sheasby, Jenny Stacey, Liz Trigg, Hilaire Walden, Laura Washburn, Steven Wheeler, Judy Williams, Polly Wreford,
Jeni Wright and Elizabeth Wolf-Cohen
Photographers: Karl Adamson, Edward Allwright, David Armstrong, Steve Baxter, James Duncan, John Freeman, Ian Garlick,
Michelle Garrett, John Heseltine, Amanda Heywood, Ferguson Hill, Janine Hosegood, David Jordan, Don Last,
William Lingwood, Patrick McLeavey, Thomas Odulate, Juliet Piddington and Peter Reilly
Designer: Carole Perks
Editorial Reader: Richard McGinlay
Production Controller: Bessie Bai

ETHICAL TRADING POLICY

Because of our ongoing ecological investment programme, you, as our customer, can have the pleasure and reassurance
of knowing that a tree is being cultivated on your behalf to naturally replace the materials used to make the book
you are holding. For further information about this scheme, go to www.annesspublishing.com/trees

A CIP catalogue record for this book is available from the British Library.

Previously published as *Hot & Spicy Chicken*

NOTES

Bracketed terms are intended for American readers.
For all recipes, quantities are given in both metric and imperial measures and, where appropriate, in standard cups
and spoons. Follow one set of measures, but not a mixture, because they are not interchangeable.
Standard spoon and cup measures are level. 1 tsp = 5ml, 1 tbsp = 15ml, 1 cup = 250ml/8fl oz.
Australian standard tablespoons are 20ml. Australian readers should use 3 tsp in place of 1 tbsp for measuring
small quantities.
American pints are 16fl oz/2 cups. American readers should use 20fl oz/2.5 cups in place of 1 pint when measuring liquids.
Electric oven temperatures in this book are for conventional ovens. When using a fan oven, the temperature will probably
need to be reduced by about 10–20°C/20–40°F. Since ovens vary, you should check with your manufacturer's
instruction book for guidance.
Medium (US large) eggs are used unless otherwise stated.

Main front cover image shows Chicken & Mushroom Donburi – for recipe, see page 84.

PUBLISHER'S NOTE

Although the advice and information in this book are believed to be accurate and true at the time of going to press,
neither the authors nor the publisher can accept any legal responsibility or liability for any errors or omissions that
may have been made nor for any inaccuracies nor for any loss, harm or injury that comes about from following
instructions or advice in this book.

Contents

Introduction

Spices were once such a precious commodity that they were used, like money, to buy land or even pay taxes. Today, clever cooks – from Thailand to Mexico and from Morocco to India – value them almost as highly. The subtle and fragrant combination of cinnamon, coriander and cumin, the colourful and peppery partnership of cayenne and paprika, the

piquant mixture of ginger, turmeric and fenugreek and the scorching heat of fresh, dried, ground or flaked chillies set the world's taste buds tingling. The versatility of chicken makes it the perfect choice for cooking with spices. A neutral and often unexciting meat, it can be transformed into an exhilarating taste experience by simple spicing.

This book is packed with inspirational recipes for lovers of lively food. There are five chapters of sizzling recipes for all occasions and courses –

and all degrees of heat. From truly warming soups to tantalize the palate to fast and furious stir-fries for a speedy midweek supper, and from well-seasoned stuffings for sophisticated roasts to devilish little morsels to serve with drinks, there is sure to be something to fire your imagination. Spices pep up salads, make snacks memorable and can turn

simple rice, pasta and noodle dishes into breathtaking feasts.

A whole chapter of recipes is devoted to the uncrowned king of all spicy dishes – the curry. Addicts can work their way through mellow and creamy Chicken Korma, lemon-scented Chicken with Ginger & Lemon Grass, sweet-and-sour Spicy Masala Chicken all the way to a

volcanic Balti Chicken Vindaloo – the hottest curry in the options.

Chicken is always a popular choice for the barbecue, and a host of easy recipes for marinades, dips and salsas will help you turn a warm evening into a hot night. Scorching barbecue favourites, such as Devilled Chicken and Caribbean Jerk Chicken, are included.

Of course, spices aren't just about making food fiery hot – they are about adding flavour, too. Matching, balancing and contrasting flavourings

are what turns good food into a great meal. The first pages of the book contain a useful guide to many popular spices and step-by-step techniques for preparing them.

So whether your tastes are for the discreetly aromatic or the tongue-blistering hot, you will be able to ignite your imagination and add relish to your culinary repertoire.

Spices & Flavourings

It is the blending of spices, seasonings and flavourings that gives food its character. The quantities specified in the recipes are merely a guide, so feel free to increase or decrease these as you wish. When devising a menu using various spices, try to balance the level of heat so that the different flavours are discernible and not swamped by one fiery spice.

Chillies & Chilli products

There are more than 200 different types of chilli, ranging in potency from the mild and flavourful to the blisteringly hot. Dried chillies tend to be hotter than fresh. Smaller chillies, such as bird's eye chillies, contain proportionately more seeds and membrane, which makes them much more potent than larger ones.

Bird's eye chillies

• Dried chilli flakes and crushed chillies contain the flesh and seeds of red chillies and can be used in their own right or as a substitute for fresh chillies.

• Cayenne pepper is an extremely hot, finely ground powder, made from a variety of red chilli. Use it in tiny amounts as a seasoning.

• Chilli powder is milder than cayenne and more coarsely ground. It is prepared from a variety of mild to hot chillies and some brands also contain other flavourings, such as cumin and oregano.

• Chilli oil is good for frying or for basting barbecued (grilled) chicken. It can also be used to add a lift to simple pasta dishes.

• Chilli paste is sold in small jars and is easy to prepare at home by processing seeded fresh chillies in a small food processor.

• Chilli sauce is used in small quantities for seasoning. Tabasco is probably the best-known brand and several kinds of Thai sweet chilli sauce are also available.

Indian Spices

The following spices are characteristic of, but not exclusive to, Indian cuisine.

• Cardamom pods are green, black and creamy beige. Whole pods, used in rice and meat dishes to add flavour, should not be eaten.

• Coriander is one of the most popular spices. The small beige seeds are used whole and ground, giving a slightly sweet flavour.

• Cumin is available as whole dark-brown or black seeds and ground. The whole seeds are often fried in oil, releasing a strong musky flavour and aroma.

Ground cumin

• Curry leaves are the Indian version of bay leaves.

• Garam masala is the main spice mixture of Indian cooking. It is a hot and aromatic powder, usually added at the end of cooking.

• Curry powder is not authentically Indian. There are many types of this spice mixture, varying in both flavour and colour.

• Fenugreek seeds are small and pungent. Use sparingly.

• Mustard seeds are added to hot oil to release a nutty flavour.

• Onion seeds are black and triangular. They are used in pickles and to flavour curries.

Fenugreek seeds

• Turmeric is a root, but is most often sold as a bright yellow powder. It is mainly used for its colouring properties and has a bitter flavour.

Nutmeg

The warm, sweet flavour of nutmeg enlivens many North African and Middle Eastern dishes. Freshly grated nutmeg is far superior to the ready-ground variety.

Cinnamon

This is available whole or ground. Sticks are used for flavouring and are not eaten. They are usually removed from the dish before serving.

Paprika

A milder relative of cayenne, paprika can be used more liberally, adding flavour as well as heat.

Cinnamon sticks, paprika, fennel seeds & cloves

Fennel Seeds

Similar to aniseed (anise seed), they are used with vegetables and meat.

Cloves

These are used in spice mixtures, such as garam masala, and in meat and rice dishes.

Peppercorns

Black peppercorns are used whole and ground.

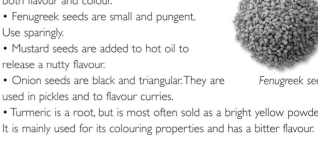

Ginger & Galangal

These pungent roots are closely related and are best used fresh, as the ground and powdered versions taste quite different. Galangal, with its fragrant, slightly peppery taste is widely used in Thai cuisine.

Ginger

Galangal

Kaffir Lime Leaves

These aromatic citrus leaves are used extensively in Thai and Indonesian cuisine.

Lemon Grass

This long fibrous stalk has a fragrant citrus aroma and flavour when cut, and is a familiar part of South-east Asian cooking.

Saffron

The world's most expensive spice is made from the dried stigmas of a crocus. Only a tiny amount of this bright-orange spice is needed to add colour and flavour.

Coriander (Cilantro)

The leaves, stems and roots of this aromatic herb are used for flavouring dishes from many cuisines.

Techniques

Grinding Spices

Whole spices freshly ground by hand, using a mortar and pestle, or an electric coffee grinder provide better flavour and aroma than ready-ground spices. Do not be tempted to grind too much, as they tend to lose their potency. Some spices, such as mace, fenugreek, cloves and turmeric, are difficult to grind at home and are better bought ready-ground.

Dry-frying Spices

This enhances the flavour and aroma of spices. Put them in a dry frying pan and cook over a low heat, shaking the pan frequently, for 1 minute or until the spices release their aroma and seeds begin to pop.

Preparing Fresh Ginger & Galangal

These can be sliced, cut into strips, finely chopped or grated.

1 Peel the skin off the root with a peeler or a small, sharp knife. Then cut into thin strips, using a large, sharp knife.

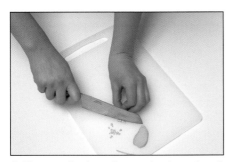

2 Place each piece flat on the board and cut into fine strips, or chop finely.

Preparing Lemon Grass

Use the whole stalk and remove it before serving, or chop finely.

1 Trim the end of the stalk and cut off the tops, leaving 10cm/4in.

2 Split in half lengthways and finely chop or, if the bulb is particularly fresh, thinly slice. Use as required.

Garam Masala

This spicy powder is added at the end of cooking.

Makes about 50g/2oz
10 dried red chillies
3 x 2.5cm/1in cinnamon sticks
2 curry leaves
30ml/2 tbsp coriander seeds
30ml/2 tbsp cumin seeds
5ml/1 tsp black peppercorns
5ml/1 tsp cloves
5ml/1 tsp fenugreek seeds
5ml/1 tsp black mustard seeds
1.5ml/ ¼ tsp chilli powder

1 Dry-fry the chillies, cinnamon and curry leaves in a heavy frying pan for 2 minutes. Add the remaining whole spices and dry-fry for 8–10 minutes, shaking the pan frequently.

2 Cool slightly, then grind to a fine powder using a coffee grinder or pestle and mortar. Mix in the chilli powder.

Preparing Chillies

Seeding chillies reduces their heat.

1 Always protect your hands, as chillies can irritate the skin. Halve each chilli lengthways and remove and discard the seeds.

2 Slice or finely chop and use as required. Always wash your hands thoroughly after preparing chillies.

Curry Paste

A "wet" blend of cooked spices, convenient for adding to recipes.

Makes about 600ml/1 pint/2½ cups
50g/2oz/ ½ cup coriander seeds
60ml/4 tbsp cumin seeds
30ml/2 tbsp fennel seeds
30ml/2 tbsp fenugreek seeds
4 dried red chillies
5 curry leaves
15ml/1 tbsp chilli powder
15ml/1 tbsp ground turmeric
150ml/ ¼ pint/ ⅔ cup white wine vinegar
250ml/8fl oz/1 cup vegetable oil

1 Grind all the whole spices to a fine powder. Spoon into a bowl and add the remaining ground spices. Mix to a thin paste with the vinegar and add 75ml/ 5 tbsp water.

2 Stir-fry the paste in the oil for 10 minutes or until the water has been absorbed. When the oil rises to the surface, the paste is cooked. Cool slightly before spooning into sterilized jars.

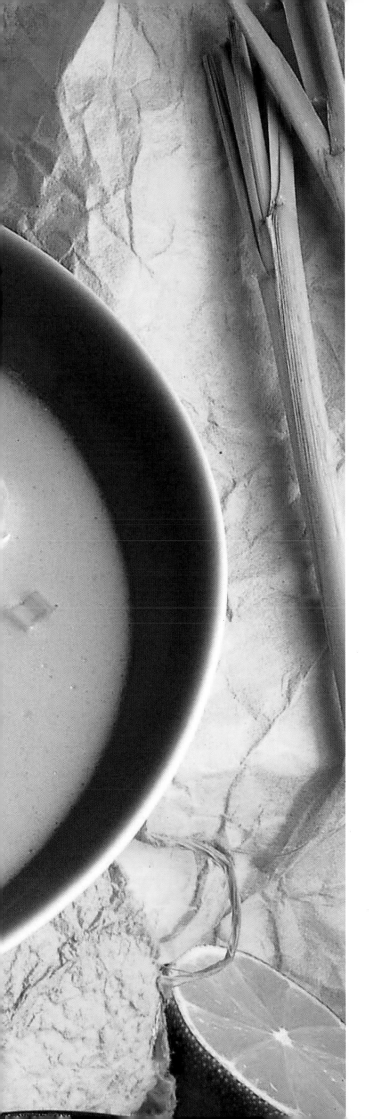

SOUPS, APPETIZERS, SNACKS & SALADS

If you want your guests to sit up and pay attention, is there a better way to start a meal than with a scorching soup, red-hot snacks or the striking contrast of a fiery spiced salad? All the recipes in this chapter are designed to set the taste buds tingling – whether they be a soup from Africa, spicy wings from the United States, Mexican tacos or a Vietnamese salad. Chicken soup is arguably the world's favourite dish, and these superb variations on the theme amply demonstrate why. Whether your taste is for the subtle and aromatic, the mild and mouthwatering or the searingly hot, you will find sizzling appetizers and snacks for every occasion. There are tempting morsels to serve with pre-dinner drinks, elegant first courses for dinner parties and substantial snacks that are almost a meal in themselves. Delicious dips, salsas and sauces either provide a cooling contrast or stoke the fire and always introduce an element of fun.

Chicken, Tomato & Christophene Soup

An unusual soup from Africa, which includes smoked haddock and christophene, a vegetable available from ethnic food shops.

Serves 4

225g/8oz skinless chicken
   breast fillets
I garlic clove, crushed
pinch of freshly grated nutmeg
25g/1oz/2 tbsp butter
   or margarine
1/2 onion, finely chopped
15ml/1 tbsp tomato
   purée (paste)
400g/14oz can tomatoes, puréed
1.2 litres/2 pints/5 cups
   chicken stock
I fresh chilli, seeded and chopped
I christophene, peeled and diced,
   about 350g/12oz
5ml/1 tsp dried oregano
2.5ml/ 1/2 tsp dried thyme
50g/2oz smoked haddock fillet,
   skinned and diced
salt and freshly ground
   black pepper
chopped fresh chives, to garnish

1 Dice the chicken, place in a bowl and season with salt, pepper, garlic and nutmeg. Mix well to flavour the chicken and then set aside for about 30 minutes.

2 Melt the butter or margarine in a large pan, add the chicken and sauté over a moderate heat for 5–6 minutes. Stir in the onion and fry gently for a further 5 minutes until the onion is slightly softened.

3 Add the tomato purée, puréed tomatoes, stock, chilli, christophene and herbs. Bring to the boil, cover and simmer gently for 35 minutes until the christophene is tender.

4 Add the smoked fish and simmer for a further 5 minutes or until the fish is cooked through. Taste the soup and adjust the seasoning as necessary. Pour into warmed soup bowls, garnish with a sprinkling of chopped chives and serve.

Tortilla Soup

You can make this Mexican-style soup as mild or as fiery as you wish.

Serves 4–6

vegetable oil, for frying
I onion, finely chopped
I large garlic clove, crushed
2 medium tomatoes, peeled,
   seeded and chopped
2.5ml/ 1/2 tsp salt
1.75 litres/3 pints/7 1/2 cups
   chicken stock
I carrot, diced
I small courgette (zucchini), diced
I chicken skinless breast fillet,
   cooked and shredded
25–50g/1–2oz canned green
   chillies, chopped

For the garnish
4 corn tortillas
I small ripe avocado
2 spring onions
   (scallions), chopped
chopped fresh coriander (cilantro)
grated Cheddar cheese (optional)

1 Heat 15ml/1 tbsp oil in a large pan. Add the onion and garlic, and cook over a medium heat for 5–8 minutes until just softened. Add the tomatoes and salt, and cook for 5 minutes more. Stir in the stock. Bring to the boil, then lower the heat and simmer, covered, for about 15 minutes.

2 Meanwhile, to make the garnish, trim the tortillas into squares, then cut them into strips. Pour 1cm/ 1/2in depth of oil into a frying pan and heat until hot but not smoking. Add the tortilla strips, in batches, and fry until just beginning to brown, turning occasionally. Remove with a slotted spoon and drain on kitchen paper.

3 Add the carrot to the soup. Cook, covered, for 10 minutes. Add the courgette, shredded chicken and green chillies, and continue cooking, uncovered, for about 5 minutes until the vegetables are just tender.

4 Meanwhile, peel and stone (pit) the avocado. Cut the flesh into fine dice. Divide the tortilla strips among warmed soup bowls. Sprinkle with the avocado. Ladle in the soup, then sprinkle the spring onions and coriander on top. Serve immediately, with grated Cheddar if you like.

Chicken & Almond Soup

This rich and creamy soup makes an excellent appetizer for an Indian meal or, served with naan bread, a satisfying and delicious lunch or supper dish.

Serves 4

75g/3oz/6 tbsp unsalted (sweet) butter
1 medium leek, chopped
2.5ml/ ½ tsp grated fresh root ginger
75g/3oz/1 cup ground almonds
5ml/1 tsp salt
2.5ml/ ½ tsp crushed black peppercorns
1 fresh green chilli, chopped
1 medium carrot, sliced
50g/2oz/ ½ cup frozen peas
115g/4oz skinless, boneless, chicken, cubed
15ml/1 tbsp chopped fresh coriander (cilantro)
450ml/¾ pint/scant 2 cups water
250ml/8fl oz/1 cup single (light) cream
4 coriander (cilantro) sprigs, to garnish

1 Melt the butter in a large karahi or deep, round-based frying pan and sauté the leek with the ginger until soft.

2 Lower the heat and add the ground almonds, salt, peppercorns, chilli, carrot, peas and chicken. Fry for about 10 minutes, or until the chicken is completely cooked, stirring constantly. Add the chopped coriander.

3 Remove from the heat and allow to cool slightly. Transfer the mixture to a food processor or blender and process for about 1½ minutes. Pour in the water and process for a further 30 seconds.

4 Pour the soup back into the pan and bring to the boil, stirring occasionally. Once it has boiled, lower the heat and gradually stir in the cream. Cook gently for a further 2 minutes, stirring occasionally.

5 Serve the soup immediately in warmed bowls, garnished with the fresh coriander sprigs.

Spicy Chicken & Mushroom Soup

A creamy chicken soup which makes a hearty meal for a winter's night. Serve it piping hot with lots of fresh garlic bread.

Serves 4

225g/8oz skinless, boneless, chicken
75g/3oz/6 tbsp unsalted (sweet) butter
2.5ml/ ½ tsp crushed garlic
5ml/1 tsp garam masala
5ml/1 tsp crushed black peppercorns
5ml/1 tsp salt
1.5ml/ ¼ tsp grated nutmeg
1 medium leek, sliced
75g/3oz/generous 1 cup mushrooms, sliced
50g/2oz/ ⅓ cup sweetcorn kernels
300ml/ ½ pint/1 ¼ cups water
250ml/8fl oz/1 cup single (light) cream
15ml/1 tbsp chopped fresh coriander (cilantro)
5ml/1 tsp crushed dried red chillies (optional)

1 Cut the chicken pieces into very fine, even-size strips.

2 Melt the butter in a medium pan. Lower the heat slightly and add the garlic and garam masala. Lower the heat even further and add the black peppercorns, salt and nutmeg. Finally add the chicken pieces, sliced leek, mushrooms and sweetcorn kernels, and cook for 5–7 minutes or until the chicken is cooked through, stirring constantly.

3 Remove from the heat and allow to cool slightly. Transfer three-quarters of the mixture into a food processor or blender. Add the water and process for about 1 minute.

4 Pour the resulting purée back into the pan with the rest of the mixture and bring to the boil over a medium heat. Lower the heat and stir in the cream.

5 Add the fresh coriander. Taste the soup and adjust the seasoning as necessary. Serve hot, garnished with the crushed red chillies if you like.

Chicken Wonton Soup with Prawns

This Indonesian version of wonton soup is more luxurious than the more widely known basic recipe and is almost a meal in itself.

Serves 4
300g/11oz skinless chicken
   breast fillet
200g/7oz prawn (shrimp) tails,
   fresh or cooked
5ml/1 tsp finely chopped fresh
   root ginger
2 spring onions (scallions),
   finely chopped
1 egg
10ml/2 tsp oyster sauce (optional)
15ml/1 tbsp cornflour
   (cornstarch)
1 packet wonton skins
900ml/1½ pints/3¾ cups
   chicken stock
¼ cucumber, peeled and diced
salt and freshly ground
   black pepper

For the garnish
1 spring onion (scallion), roughly
   shredded
4 sprigs coriander (cilantro) leaves
1 tomato, peeled, seeded
   and diced

1 Place the chicken breast, 150g/5oz of the prawn tails, the ginger and spring onions in a food processor and process for 2–3 minutes. Add the egg, oyster sauce (if using) and seasoning and process briefly. Set aside.

2 Mix the cornflour with a little water to form a thin paste. Place 8 wonton skins at a time on a work surface, moisten the edges with the cornflour paste and place 2.5ml/ ½ tsp of the filling in the middle of each. Fold each wonton in half and pinch to seal.

3 Bring the chicken stock to the boil, add the remaining prawn tails and the cucumber, and simmer for 3–4 minutes. Add the wontons and simmer to warm through.

4 Ladle the soup into warmed bowls and garnish with shredded spring onion, coriander leaves and diced tomato. Serve immediately in warmed bowls.

Chicken Mulligatawny

Using the original pepper water – mulla-ga-tani – this famous dish was created by the non-vegetarian chefs during the British Raj and imported to the United Kingdom.

Serves 4–6
900g/2lb boneless, skinless
   chicken, cubed
600ml/1 pint/2½ cups water
6 green cardamom pods
5cm/2in cinnamon stick
4–6 curry leaves
15ml/1 tbsp ground coriander
5ml/1 tsp ground cumin
2.5ml/½ tsp ground turmeric
3 garlic cloves, crushed
12 peppercorns
4 cloves
1 onion, finely chopped
115g/4oz coconut cream block
juice of 2 lemons
salt
deep-fried onions and chopped
   fresh coriander (cilantro),
   to garnish

1 Place the chicken in a large pan with the water and cook until tender. Skim the surface, then strain, reserving the stock. Keep the chicken warm.

2 Return the stock to the pan and reheat. Add the cardamom, cinnamon, curry leaves, ground coriander, cumin and turmeric, garlic, peppercorns, cloves and onion. Add the creamed coconut, grated or chopped if you wish, the lemon juice and salt to taste. Simmer for 10–15 minutes.

3 Strain the soup again and return the chicken to the pan. Simmer for a few minutes to reheat thoroughly.

4 Taste the soup and adjust the seasoning as necessary. Divide among warmed bowls, garnish with deep-fried onions and chopped fresh coriander and serve.

Thai-style Chicken Soup

A fragrant blend of coconut milk, lemon grass, ginger and lime makes a delicious soup, with just a hint of chilli.

Serves 4

5ml/1 tsp oil
1–2 fresh red chillies, seeded and chopped
2 garlic cloves, crushed
1 large leek, thinly sliced
600ml/1 pint/2½ cups chicken stock
400ml/14fl oz/1⅔ cups coconut milk
450g/1lb boneless, skinless chicken thighs, cut into bitesize pieces
30ml/2 tbsp Thai fish sauce (nam pla)
1 lemon grass stalk, split
2.5cm/1in piece fresh root ginger, peeled and finely chopped
5ml/1 tsp sugar
4 kaffir lime leaves (optional)
75g/3oz/¾ cup frozen peas, thawed
45ml/3 tbsp chopped fresh coriander (cilantro)

1 Heat the oil in a large pan, and cook the chillies and garlic for about 2 minutes. Add the leek and cook for a further 2 minutes.

2 Stir in the stock and coconut milk, and bring to the boil.

3 Add the chicken, with the fish sauce, lemon grass, ginger, sugar and lime leaves, if using. Simmer, covered, for 15 minutes or until the chicken is tender, stirring occasionally.

4 Add the peas and cook for a further 3 minutes until heated through. Remove the lemon grass and stir in the coriander just before serving.

> **Cook's Tip**
> *Kaffir lime leaves are aromatic and used frequently in South-east Asian cooking. They are available from specialist shops.*

Spiced Vegetable Soup with Chicken & Prawns

Aubergine, green beans, red pepper, cabbage, succulent chicken and prawns are given a truly exotic flavour with a fabulous mixture of spices.

Serves 6–8

1 onion
2 garlic cloves, crushed
1 fresh red or green chilli, seeded and sliced
1cm/½in cube shrimp paste
3 macadamia nuts or 6 almonds
1cm/½in piece galangal, peeled and sliced
5ml/1 tsp sugar
oil, for frying
225g/8oz skinless chicken breast fillet, cut into 1cm/½in cubes
300ml/½ pint/1¼ cups coconut milk
1.2 litres/2 pints/5 cups chicken stock
1 aubergine (eggplant), diced
225g/8oz green beans, chopped
small wedge of white cabbage, shredded
1 red (bell) pepper, seeded and finely sliced
115g/4oz cooked peeled prawns (shrimp)
salt and freshly ground black pepper

1 Halve the onion; slice one half and set aside; cut the other half in two and place in a mortar. Add the garlic, chilli, shrimp paste, nuts, galangal and sugar, and grind to a paste using a pestle. Alternatively, grind in a food processor.

2 Heat a wok, add the oil and fry the paste, without browning, until it gives off a rich aroma. Add the reserved onion and chicken, and cook for 3–4 minutes. Stir in the coconut milk and stock. Bring to the boil and simmer for a few minutes. Add the aubergine and beans, and cook for only a few minutes until the beans are almost tender.

3 A few minutes before serving, stir in the cabbage, pepper and prawns. The vegetables should be cooked so that they are still crunchy and the prawns merely heated through. Taste the soup and adjust the seasoning as necessary. Serve in warmed bowls.

Ginger, Chicken & Coconut Soup

The ginger flavour in this aromatic soup is provided by galangal, which belongs to the same family as the more familiar fresh root ginger.

Serves 4–6
750ml/1¼ pints/3 cups
    coconut milk
475ml/16fl oz/2 cups
    chicken stock
4 lemon grass stalks, bruised
    and chopped
2.5cm/1in piece galangal,
    thinly sliced

10 black peppercorns, crushed
10 kaffir lime leaves, torn
300g/11oz boneless chicken, cut
    into thin strips
115g/4oz/1½ cups
    button (white) mushrooms
50g/2oz/½ cup baby sweetcorn
60ml/4 tbsp lime juice
45ml/3 tbsp Thai fish sauce
    (nam pla)

For the garnish
2 fresh red chillies, chopped
a few spring onions
    (scallions), chopped
fresh coriander (cilantro) leaves

1 Bring the coconut milk and chicken stock to the boil in a medium pan. Add the lemon grass, galangal, peppercorns and half the kaffir lime leaves, reduce the heat and simmer gently for 10 minutes.

2 Strain the stock into a clean pan. Return to the heat, then add the chicken, button mushrooms and baby sweetcorn. Simmer for about 5–7 minutes or until the chicken is cooked.

3 Stir in the lime juice, fish sauce to taste and the rest of the kaffir lime leaves.

4 Serve the soup hot in warmed bowls, garnished with chopped fresh red chillies, spring onions and coriander.

Chiang Mai Noodle Soup

A signature dish of the Thai city of Chiang Mai, this delicious noodle soup, in fact, has Burmese origins.

Serves 4–6
600ml/1 pint/2½ cups
    coconut milk
30ml/2 tbsp red curry paste
5ml/1 tsp ground turmeric
450g/1lb boneless chicken thighs,
    cut into bitesize chunks
600ml/1 pint/2½ cups
    chicken stock
60ml/4 tbsp Thai fish sauce
15ml/1 tbsp dark soy sauce

juice of ½–1 lime
450g/1lb fresh egg noodles,
    blanched briefly in boiling water
salt and freshly ground
    black pepper

For the garnish
3 spring onions
    (scallions), chopped
4 fresh red chillies, chopped
4 shallots, chopped
60ml/4 tbsp sliced pickled
    mustard leaves, rinsed
30ml/2 tbsp fried sliced garlic
fresh coriander (cilantro) leaves
4 fried noodle nests (optional)

1 Pour about one-third of the coconut milk into a large pan and bring to the boil, stirring often with a wooden spoon until it separates.

2 Add the curry paste and ground turmeric, stir to mix completely and cook gently until fragrant.

3 Add the chicken and stir-fry for about 2 minutes, ensuring that all the chunks are coated with the paste.

4 Add the remaining coconut milk, the chicken stock, fish sauce and soy sauce. Season with salt and pepper to taste. Simmer over a low heat for 7–10 minutes. Remove from the heat and stir in the lime juice.

5 Reheat the noodles in boiling water, drain and divide among warmed individual bowls. Divide the chicken between the bowls and ladle in the hot soup. Top each bowl with a few of each of the garnishes and serve.

Tandoori Chicken Sticks

This aromatic chicken dish is traditionally baked in a clay oven called a tandoor.

Makes about 25
450g/1lb skinless chicken
   breast fillets

**For the coriander
(cilantro) yogurt**
250ml/8fl oz/1 cup natural
   (plain) yogurt
30ml/2 tbsp whipping cream
1/2 cucumber, peeled, seeded and
   finely chopped
15–30ml/1–2 tbsp chopped fresh
   coriander (cilantro) or mint
salt and freshly ground
   black pepper

For the marinade
175ml/6fl oz/ 3/4 cup natural
   (plain) yogurt
5ml/1 tsp garam masala or
   curry powder
1.25ml/ 1/4 tsp ground cumin
1.25ml/ 1/4 tsp ground coriander
1.25ml/ 1/4 tsp cayenne pepper
   (or to taste)
5ml/1 tsp tomato purée (paste)
1–2 garlic cloves, finely chopped
2.5cm/ 1/2in piece fresh root
   ginger, peeled and
   finely chopped
grated rind and juice of
   1/2 lemon
15–30ml/1–2 tbsp chopped fresh
   coriander (cilantro) or mint

1 First, make the coriander yogurt. Mix all the ingredients and season with salt and pepper. Cover and chill.

2 To make the marinade, place all the ingredients in a food processor and process until smooth. Pour into a shallow dish.

3 Freeze the chicken fillets for 5 minutes to firm them, then slice in half horizontally. Cut the slices into 2cm/3/4in strips and add to the marinade. Toss to coat well. Cover and chill for 6–8 hours or overnight.

4 Preheat the grill (broiler) and line a baking sheet with foil. Using a slotted spoon, remove the chicken from the marinade and arrange the pieces in a single layer on the baking sheet. Scrunch them up slightly to make wavy shapes. Grill (broil) for 4–5 minutes until brown and just cooked, turning once. Thread 1–2 pieces of cooked chicken on to cocktail sticks or short skewers and serve with the bowl of coriander yogurt.

Sesame Seed Chicken Bites

Best served warm, these crunchy bites are delicious accompanied by a glass of chilled dry white wine.

Makes 20
175g/6oz chicken breast fillet
2 garlic cloves, crushed
2.5cm/1in piece fresh root ginger,
   peeled and grated
1 small (US medium) egg white
5ml/1 tsp cornflour (cornstarch)
25g/1oz/ 1/4 cup shelled pistachio
   nuts, roughly chopped

60ml/4 tbsp sesame seeds
30ml/2 tbsp grapeseed oil
salt and freshly ground
   black pepper

For the dipping sauce
45ml/3 tbsp hoisin sauce
15ml/1 tbsp sweet chilli sauce

For the garnish
finely shredded fresh root ginger
roughly chopped pistachio nuts
fresh dill sprigs

1 Place the chicken, garlic, grated ginger, egg white and cornflour in a food processor, and process to a smooth paste. Stir in the pistachio nuts, and season well with salt and freshly ground black pepper.

2 Place the sesame seeds in a bowl. Form the chicken mixture into 20 balls between the palms of the hands and roll in the sesame seeds to coat them completely.

3 Heat a wok and add the oil. When the oil is hot, stir-fry the chicken bites, in batches, turning regularly until golden. Drain on kitchen paper and keep warm.

4 To make the dipping sauce, mix together the hoisin and chilli sauces in a small bowl.

5 Place the chicken bites on a serving platter and garnish with shredded ginger, chopped pistachio nuts and dill. Serve with the dipping sauce.

Thai-style Chicken Livers

This dish is full of the flavours of Thailand.

Serves 4–6
45ml/3 tbsp vegetable oil
450g/1lb chicken livers, trimmed
4 shallots, chopped
2 garlic cloves, chopped
15ml/1 tbsp roasted ground rice
45ml/3 tbsp Thai fish sauce
45ml/3 tbsp lime juice
5ml/1 tsp sugar
2 lemon grass stalks, bruised and finely chopped
30ml/2 tbsp chopped fresh coriander (cilantro)
10–12 fresh mint leaves and 2 fresh red chillies, chopped, to garnish

1 Heat the oil in a wok or large frying pan. Add the livers and fry over a medium-high heat for about 4 minutes until the livers are golden brown and cooked, but still slightly pink inside.

2 Move the livers to one side of the pan, and add the shallots and garlic. Fry for about 1–2 minutes.

3 Add the ground rice, fish sauce, lime juice, sugar, lemon grass and coriander. Stir, remove from the heat, and discard the lemon grass. Serve garnished with mint leaves and chillies.

Chicken Livers with Chinese Chives

This popular Thai dish is simplicity itself.

Serves 4
450g/1lb chicken livers, trimmed
3 garlic cloves, finely chopped
45ml/3 tbsp groundnut (peanut) oil
450g/1lb Chinese chives, cut into 4cm/1½in lengths
15–30ml/2–3 tbsp Thai fish sauce
30ml/2 tbsp oyster sauce
15ml/1 tbsp sugar

1 Cut the livers into thin strips using a sharp knife.
2 Stir-fry the garlic in the oil for 1–2 minutes until golden. Add the livers and stir-fry over a high heat for 3–4 minutes. Add the Chinese chives, fish and oyster sauces and sugar, and cook for 1 minute more.

Spiced Chicken Livers

Chicken livers combine brilliantly with ground coriander, cumin, cardamom, paprika and nutmeg to make this tasty first course or light meal.

Serves 4
350g/12oz chicken livers, trimmed
115g/4oz/1 cup plain (all-purpose) flour
2.5ml/½ tsp ground coriander
2.5ml/½ tsp ground cumin
2.5ml/½ tsp ground cardamom seeds
1.25ml/¼ tsp ground paprika
1.25ml/¼ tsp grated nutmeg
90ml/6 tbsp olive oil
salt and freshly ground black pepper
salad and garlic bread, to serve

1 Dry the chicken livers on kitchen paper. Cut any large livers in half and leave the smaller ones whole.

2 Mix the flour with the coriander, cumin, cardamom, paprika, nutmeg, salt and pepper.

3 Coat a small batch of livers with spiced flour, separating each piece. Heat the oil in a large frying pan and fry the livers in batches. (This helps to keep the oil temperature high and prevents the flour from becoming soggy.)

4 Fry quickly, stirring frequently, until crispy. Keep warm and repeat with the remaining livers. Serve immediately with salad and warm garlic bread.

> **Cook's Tip**
> *Although always milder than chilli or cayenne pepper, paprika varies in strength from mild (sometimes called sweet) to hot.*

Chicken Kofta Balti with Paneer

This rather unusual appetizer looks most elegant when served in small individual karahis.

Serves 6
450g/1lb skinless, boneless chicken, cubed
5ml/1 tsp crushed garlic
5ml/1 tsp grated fresh root ginger
7.5ml/1 1/2 tsp ground coriander
7.5ml/1 1/2 tsp chilli powder
2.5ml/1/2 tsp ground fenugreek
1.5ml/1/4 tsp ground turmeric
5ml/1 tsp salt
30ml/2 tbsp chopped fresh coriander (cilantro)
2 fresh green chillies, chopped
600ml/1 pint/2 1/2 cups water
corn oil, for frying
1 dried red chilli, crushed (optional), and fresh mint sprigs, to garnish

For the paneer mixture
1 medium onion, sliced
1 red (bell) pepper, seeded and cut into strips
1 green (bell) pepper, seeded and cut into strips
175g/6oz paneer, cubed
175g/6oz/1 cup sweetcorn kernels

1 Put the chicken, garlic, spices, salt, fresh coriander, fresh green chillies and water into a medium pan. Bring slowly to the boil over a medium heat and cook until all the liquid has evaporated.

2 Remove from the heat and allow to cool slightly. Put the mixture into a food processor or blender and process for 2 minutes, stopping once or twice to loosen the mixture with a spoon or spatula.

3 Scrape the mixture into a large mixing bowl using a wooden spoon. Taking a little of the mixture at a time, shape it into small even-size balls using your hands. You should be able to make about 12 koftas.

4 Heat 1cm/1/2in oil in a karahi or deep, round-based frying pan over a high heat. Turn the heat down slightly and drop the koftas carefully into the oil. Move them around gently to ensure that they cook evenly.

5 When the koftas are lightly browned, remove them from the oil with a slotted spoon and drain on kitchen paper. Set aside.

6 Reheat the oil still remaining in the karahi and flash fry all the ingredients for the paneer mixture. This should take about 3 minutes over a high heat.

7 Divide the paneer mixture evenly between 6 small individual karahis, if using. Add 2 koftas to each serving and garnish with crushed red chilli, if using, and mint sprigs.

Cook's Tip
Paneer is a smooth white cheese available from Asian foodstores and some supermarkets.

Buffalo-style Chicken Wings

A fiery-hot fried chicken recipe, said to have originated in the town of Buffalo, New York, after which it is named. Serve it with traditional blue-cheese dip and celery sticks.

Makes 48
24 chicken wings, tips removed
vegetable oil, for frying
75g/3oz/6 tbsp butter
50ml/2oz/1/4 cup hot pepper sauce, or to taste
15ml/1 tbsp white or cider vinegar
salt
salad leaves, to garnish
celery sticks, to serve

For the blue-cheese dip
115g/4oz blue cheese, such as Danish blue
120ml/4fl oz/1/2 cup mayonnaise
120ml/4fl oz/1/2 cup sour cream
2–3 spring onions (scallions), finely chopped
1 garlic clove, finely chopped
15ml/1 tbsp white or cider vinegar

1 To make the dip, use a fork to mash the blue cheese gently against the side of a bowl. Add the mayonnaise, sour cream, spring onions, garlic and vinegar, and stir together until well blended. Chill until ready to serve.

2 Using kitchen scissors or a sharp knife, cut each wing in half at the joint to make 48 pieces in all.

3 In a large pan or wok, heat 5cm/2in of oil until hot but not smoking. Fry the chicken wing pieces, in small batches, for 8–10 minutes until crisp and golden, turning once. Drain on kitchen paper. Season with salt to taste and arrange in a bowl.

4 In a pan over a medium-low heat, melt the butter. Stir in the hot pepper sauce and vinegar, and immediately pour over the chicken, tossing to combine. Serve the wings hot, garnished with salad leaves and accompanied by the blue- cheese dip and celery sticks.

Bon-bon Chicken with Sesame Sauce

For this popular Sichuan Chinese dish, the chicken meat is tenderized by being beaten with a stick (called a *bon*) – hence its name.

Serves 6–8
1 chicken, about 1 kg/2¼lb
1.2 litres/2 pints/5 cups water
15ml/1 tbsp sesame oil
shredded cucumber, to garnish

For the sauce
30ml/2 tbsp light soy sauce
5ml/1 tsp sugar
15ml/1 tbsp finely chopped
   spring onions (scallions)
5ml/1 tsp red chilli oil
2.5ml/½ tsp ground
   Sichuan peppercorns
5ml/1 tsp white sesame seeds
10ml/2 tbsp sesame paste or
   30ml/2 tbsp peanut butter
   creamed with a little
   sesame oil

1 Clean the chicken well. In a wok or pan, bring the water to a rolling boil, add the chicken, reduce the heat and cook, covered, for 40–45 minutes. Remove the chicken from the pan and immerse in cold water to cool.

2 After at least 1 hour, remove the chicken from the water and drain; dry well with kitchen paper and brush on a coating of sesame oil. Carve the meat off the legs, wings and breast, and pull the meat off the rest of the bones.

3 On a flat work surface, pound the meat with a rolling pin, then tear it into shreds with your fingers.

4 To make the sauce, mix together all the ingredients in a bowl, reserving a little chopped spring onion for the garnish.

5 Place the shredded chicken in a serving dish and arrange the cucumber around the edge. Pour the sauce over the chicken, garnish with the reserved spring onion and serve.

Lettuce Parcels

This popular "assemble-it-yourself" treat is based on a recipe from Hong Kong. The filling – an imaginative blend of textures and flavours – is served with crisp lettuce leaves, which are used as wrappers.

Serves 6
2 chicken breast fillets, about
   350g/12oz total weight
4 Chinese dried mushrooms,
   soaked for 30 minutes in warm
   water to cover
vegetable oil, for stir-frying and
   deep-frying

2 garlic cloves, crushed
6 canned water chestnuts, drained
   and thinly sliced
30ml/2 tbsp light soy sauce
5ml/1 tsp Sichuan peppercorns,
   dry-fried and crushed
4 spring onions (scallions),
   finely chopped
5ml/1 tsp sesame oil
50g/2oz cellophane noodles
salt and freshly ground
   black pepper
1 crisp lettuce and 60ml/4 tbsp
   hoisin sauce, to serve

1 Remove the skin from the chicken fillets, pat dry and set aside. Cut the chicken into thin strips. Drain the soaked mushrooms. Cut off and discard the mushroom stalks; slice the caps finely and set aside.

2 Heat 30ml/2 tbsp of the oil in a wok or large frying pan. Add the garlic, then add the chicken and stir-fry until the pieces are cooked through and no longer pink.

3 Add the sliced mushrooms, water chestnuts, light soy sauce and crushed Sichuan peppercorns. Toss for 2–3 minutes, then taste and add salt and pepper if necessary. Stir in half of the spring onions and the sesame oil. Remove from the heat and set aside.

4 Heat the oil for deep-frying to 190°C/375°F. Cut the chicken skin into strips, deep-fry until very crisp and drain on kitchen paper. Add the noodles to the hot oil and deep-fry until crisp. Transfer to a plate lined with kitchen paper.

5 Crush the noodles and place in a serving dish. Top with the chicken skin, chicken and vegetable mixture and the remaining spring onions. Wash the lettuce leaves, pat dry and arrange on a large platter.

6 Toss the chicken and noodles to mix. Invite guests to take one or two lettuce leaves, spread the inside with hoisin sauce and add a spoonful of filling, turning in the sides of the leaves and rolling them into a parcel. The parcels are traditionally eaten in the hand.

> **Cook's Tip**
> *Sichuan peppercorns are wild red peppers from Sichuan province in China. They are more aromatic but less hot than either white or black peppercorns, yet give a unique flavour.*

Chicken & Sticky Rice Balls

These balls can either be steamed or deep-fried. The fried versions are crunchy and are excellent for serving at drinks parties.

Makes about 30
450g/1lb minced (ground) chicken
1 egg
15ml/1 tbsp tapioca flour
4 spring onions (scallions), finely chopped
30ml/2 tbsp chopped fresh coriander (cilantro)
30ml/2 tbsp Thai fish sauce (nam pla)
pinch of granulated sugar
225g/8oz cooked sticky rice
banana leaves
oil, for brushing
freshly ground black pepper
shredded carrot, strips of red (bell) pepper and chopped fresh chives, to garnish
sweet chilli sauce, to serve

1 In a bowl, combine the chicken, egg, flour, spring onions and coriander . Mix and season with fish sauce, sugar and pepper.

2 Spread the cooked sticky rice on a large plate or flat tray. Place 5ml/1 tsp of the chicken mixture on the bed of rice. With damp hands, roll and shape the mixture in the rice to make a ball about the size of a walnut. Repeat using the rest of the chicken mixture and rice.

3 Line a bamboo steamer with banana leaves and lightly brush them with oil. Place the chicken balls on the leaves, spacing them well apart to prevent them from sticking together. Steam over a high heat for about 10 minutes or until cooked.

4 Transfer the balls to a serving plates. Garnish with the carrot, pepper and chives. Serve with sweet chilli sauce.

Cook's Tip
Sticky rice, also known as glutinous rice, has a very high starch content. It is so called because the grains stick together when it is cooked. It is very popular in Thailand and can be eaten both as a savoury and as a sweet dish.

San Francisco Chicken Wings

A mouthwatering dish that reflects the influence of Chinese immigrants on American cuisine.

Serves 8
75ml/5 tbsp soy sauce
15ml/1 tbsp light brown sugar
15ml/1 tbsp rice vinegar
30ml/2 tbsp dry sherry
juice of 1 orange
5cm/2in strip orange rind
1 star anise
5ml/1 tsp cornflour (cornstarch)
50ml/2fl oz/ 1/4 cup water
15ml/1 tbsp grated fresh root ginger
15ml/1 tbsp crushed garlic
1.5–5ml/ 1/4–1 tsp chilli sauce
24 chicken wings, about 1.5kg/3–3 1/2lb, tips removed
salad leaves and chives, to garnish

1 Preheat the oven to 200°C/400°F/Gas 6. Combine the soy sauce, brown sugar, vinegar, sherry, orange juice and rind, and star anise in a pan. Bring to the boil over a medium heat.

2 Combine the cornflour and water in a small bowl and stir until blended. Add to the boiling soy sauce mixture, stirring well. Boil for 1 minute, stirring constantly.

3 Remove the soy sauce mixture from the heat and stir in the ginger, garlic and chilli sauce.

4 Arrange the chicken wings, in a single layer, in a large ovenproof dish. Pour over the soy sauce mixture and stir thoroughly to coat the wings evenly.

5 Bake the wings for 30–40 minutes until tender and browned, basting occasionally. Serve hot or warm, garnished with salad leaves and chives.

Mixed Tostadas

Like little edible plates, these fried Mexican tortillas can support any filling that is not too juicy.

Makes 14

oil, for shallow frying
14 freshly prepared unbaked
  corn tortillas
225g/8oz/1 cup mashed cooked
  or canned red kidney or
  pinto beans
1 Iceberg lettuce, shredded
vinaigrette dressing (optional)
2 cooked skinless chicken breast
  fillets, thinly sliced
225g/8oz ready-made guacamole
115g/4oz/1 cup coarsely grated
  Cheddar cheese
pickled jalapeño chillies, seeded
  and sliced, to taste

1 Heat the oil in a frying pan and fry the tortillas until golden brown on both sides and crisp but not hard.

2 Spread each tortilla with a layer of mashed beans. Put a layer of shredded lettuce (which can be left plain or lightly tossed with a little dressing) over the beans.

3 Arrange pieces of chicken in a layer on top of the lettuce. Carefully spread over a layer of the guacamole and finally sprinkle with the grated cheese. Sprinkle sliced pickled chillies over the top, to taste.

4 Arrange the mixed tostadas on a large serving platter. Serve on individual plates but eat using your hands.

Cook's Tip
To make a vinaigrette dressing, whisk together 45ml/3 tbsp wine vinegar, 15ml/1 tbsp Dijon mustard, and salt and pepper to taste. Gradually whisk in 150ml/¼ pint/⅔ cup olive oil. Alternatively, put all the ingredients in a screw-top jar and shake vigorously until thoroughly combined.

Mexican Chicken

Warm taco shells filled with chicken in a spicy sauce, served with lettuce, tomatoes, sour cream and grated cheese.

Serves 4

1.3kg/3lb chicken
5ml/1 tsp salt
12 taco shells
1 small Iceberg lettuce, shredded
175g/6oz tomatoes, chopped
250ml/8fl oz/1 cup sour cream
115g/4oz/1 cup grated
  Cheddar cheese

For the sauce
250ml/8fl oz/1 cup fresh
  tomatoes, peeled, cooked
  and sieved
1–2 garlic cloves, crushed
2.5ml/½ tsp cider vinegar
2.5ml/½ tsp dried oregano
2.5ml/½ tsp ground cumin
15–30ml/1–2 tbsp mild
  chilli powder

1 Put the chicken in a large pan, and add the salt and enough water to cover. Bring to the boil. Reduce the heat and simmer for about 45 minutes to 1 hour until the chicken is thoroughly cooked. Remove the chicken from the pan and allow to cool. Reserve 120ml/4fl oz/½ cup of the stock for the sauce.

2 Remove the chicken meat from the bones, discarding all the skin. Chop the meat coarsely.

3 To make the sauce, combine all the ingredients with the reserved chicken stock in a pan and bring to the boil. Stir in the chicken meat. Simmer for about 20 minutes until the sauce thickens considerably, stirring from time to time.

4 Preheat the oven to 180°C/350°F/Gas 4. Spread out the taco shells on two baking sheets and heat in the oven for 7 minutes.

5 Meanwhile, put the shredded lettuce, chopped tomatoes, sour cream and grated cheese in individual serving dishes. To serve, spoon a little of the hot chicken mixture into each taco shell. Garnish with the lettuce, tomatoes, sour cream and grated Cheddar cheese.

Tortilla Flutes

These crisply fried rolled tortillas, stuffed with chicken in fresh tomato sauce, look as good as they taste.

Makes about 12

24 freshly prepared unbaked
    flour tortillas
2 tomatoes, peeled, seeded
    and chopped
1 small onion, chopped
1 garlic clove, chopped
30–45ml/2–3 tbsp corn oil
2 freshly cooked chicken breast
    fillets, skinned and shredded
salt

For the garnish

sliced radishes
stuffed green olives
fresh coriander (cilantro)

1 Place the unbaked flour tortillas in pairs on a work surface, with the right-hand tortilla overlapping the left-hand one by about 5cm/2in.

2 Put the tomatoes, onion and garlic into a food processor and process to a purée (paste). Season with salt to taste.

3 Heat 15ml/1 tbsp of the corn oil in a frying pan and cook the tomato purée for a few minutes, stirring constantly to blend the flavours. Remove from the heat and stir in the shredded chicken, mixing well.

4 Spread about 30ml/2 tbsp of the chicken mixture on each pair of tortillas, roll them up into flutes and secure with a cocktail stick or toothpick.

5 Heat a little more of the oil in a frying pan large enough to hold the flutes comfortably. Cook more than one at a time if possible, but don't overcrowd the pan. Fry the flutes until light brown all over. Add more oil if needed.

6 Drain the cooked flutes on kitchen paper and keep hot. When ready to serve, transfer to a platter and garnish with radishes, olives and coriander.

Chicken Fajitas

Fajitas are warmed soft tortillas, filled and folded like an envelope. They are traditional Mexican fast food, delicious and easy to prepare, and a favourite for family supper.

Serves 4

115g/4oz/generous ½ cup long
    grain rice
15g/1oz/3 tbsp wild rice
15ml/1 tbsp olive oil
15ml/1 tbsp sunflower oil
1 onion, cut into thin wedges
4 chicken skinless breast fillets,
    cut into thin strips
1 red (bell) pepper, seeded and
    thinly sliced
5ml/1 tsp ground cumin
generous pinch of cayenne pepper
2.5ml/½ tsp ground turmeric
175ml/6fl oz/¾ cup passata
    (bottled strained tomatoes)
120–175ml/4–6fl oz/½–¾ cup
    chicken stock
12 small or 8 large wheat
    tortillas, warmed
sour cream, to serve

For the salsa

1 shallot, roughly chopped
1 small garlic clove
½–1 fresh green chilli, seeded and
    roughly chopped
small bunch of fresh parsley
5 tomatoes, peeled, seeded
    and chopped
10ml/2 tsp olive oil
15ml/1 tbsp lemon juice
30ml/2 tbsp tomato juice
salt and freshly ground
    black pepper

For the guacamole

1 large ripe avocado
2 spring onions
    (scallions), chopped
15–30ml/1–2 tbsp fresh lime or
    lemon juice
generous pinch of cayenne pepper
15ml/1 tbsp chopped
    fresh coriander (cilantro)

1 Cook the long grain and wild rice separately, following the instructions on the packets. Drain and set aside.

2 To make the salsa, finely chop the shallot, garlic, chilli and parsley in a blender or food processor. Spoon into a bowl. Stir in the tomatoes, olive oil, lemon juice and tomato juice. Season to taste with salt and pepper. Cover with clear film (plastic wrap) and chill.

3 To make the guacamole, scoop the avocado flesh into a bowl. Mash it lightly with the spring onions, citrus juice, cayenne, fresh coriander and seasoning, so that small pieces still remain. Cover the surface closely with clear film and chill.

4 Heat the olive and sunflower oils in a frying pan and fry the onion wedges for 4–5 minutes until softened. Add the chicken strips and pepper slices, and fry until evenly browned. Stir in the cumin, cayenne and turmeric. Fry, stirring, for 1 minute, then stir in the passata and stock. Bring to the boil, then lower the heat and simmer gently for 5–6 minutes until the chicken is cooked through. Season to taste with salt and freshly ground black pepper.

5 Stir both types of rice into the chicken and cook for 1–2 minutes until the rice is warmed through. Spoon a little of the chicken mixture on to each warmed tortilla. Top with salsa, guacamole and sour cream, and roll up.

Enchiladas with Hot Chilli Sauce

By Mexican standards, this is a low-heat version of the popular chicken enchiladas. If you like your food hot, you can add extra chillies to the sauce.

Serves 4
butter, for greasing
8 wheat tortillas
175g/6oz/1½ cups grated
   Cheddar cheese
1 onion, finely chopped
350g/12oz cooked chicken, cut
   into small chunks

300ml/ ½ pint/1¼ cups
   sour cream
1 avocado, sliced and tossed in
   lemon juice, to garnish

For the salsa picante
1–2 fresh green chillies
15ml/1 tbsp vegetable oil
1 onion, chopped
1 garlic clove, crushed
400g/14oz can
   chopped tomatoes
30ml/2 tbsp tomato
   purée (paste)
salt and freshly ground
   black pepper

1 To make the salsa picante, halve the chillies, and remove the seeds. Slice the chillies very thinly. Heat the oil in a frying pan, and fry the onion and garlic for 3–4 minutes until softened. Add the tomatoes, tomato purée and chillies. Simmer gently, uncovered, for about 12–15 minutes, stirring frequently.

2 Pour the sauce into a food processor or blender and process until smooth. Return to the heat and cook very gently, uncovered, for a further 15 minutes. Season and set aside.

3 Preheat the oven to 180°C/350°F/Gas 4 and butter a shallow, ovenproof dish. Sprinkle each tortilla with grated cheese and chopped onion, about 40g/1½oz of the chicken and 15ml/1 tbsp of the salsa. Pour over 15ml/1 tbsp of the sour cream, roll up and place, seam side down, in the dish.

4 Pour the remaining salsa picante over the top of the enchiladas and sprinkle with the remaining cheese and onion. Bake for about 25–30 minutes until the top is golden. Serve with the remaining sour cream either poured over or in a separate bowl, and garnish with the sliced avocado.

Turkey-chorizo Tacos

Chopped spicy chorizo sausage and minced turkey make a warming filling for Mexican taco shells.

Serves 4
15ml/1 tbsp vegetable oil
450g/1lb minced (ground) turkey
5ml/1 tsp salt
5ml/1 tsp ground cumin
12 taco shells

75g/3oz chorizo, finely chopped
3 spring onions
   (scallions), chopped
2 tomatoes, chopped
1 small lettuce, shredded
115g/4oz/2 cups grated
   Cheddar cheese
tomato salsa and guacamole,
   to serve

1 Preheat the oven to 180°C/350°F/Gas 4. Heat the oil in a non-stick frying pan and add the turkey, salt and cumin. Sauté over a medium heat for 5–8 minutes until the turkey is cooked through, stirring frequently to break up any lumps.

2 Meanwhile, arrange the taco shells in one layer on a large baking sheet and heat in the oven about 10 minutes or according to the directions on the package, until they are warmed through.

3 Add the chopped chorizo and spring onions to the turkey, and stir to mix. Cook until just warmed through, stirring the mixture occasionally.

4 To assemble each taco, place 1–2 spoonfuls of the turkey mixture in the base of a warmed taco shell. Top with a generous sprinkling of chopped tomato, shredded lettuce and grated cheese.

5 Serve immediately, with tomato salsa and guacamole.

Variation
You can use minced (ground) chicken instead of turkey for these tacos, if preferred.

Chicken, Vegetable & Chilli Salad

This Vietnamese salad is full of surprising textures and flavours. Serve it as a light lunch dish or for supper with crusty French bread.

Serves 4

225g/8oz Chinese
    leaves (Chinese cabbage)
2 carrots, cut into matchsticks
1/2 cucumber, cut into matchsticks
2 fresh red chillies, seeded and
    cut into thin strips
1 small onion, sliced into thin rings
4 pickled gherkins, sliced, plus
    45ml/3 tbsp of the liquid
50g/2oz/ 1/2 cup peanuts,
    lightly ground
225g/8oz cooked chicken,
    thinly sliced
1 garlic clove, crushed
5ml/1 tsp sugar
30ml/2 tbsp cider or
    white wine vinegar
salt

1 Thinly slice the Chinese leaves and spread out on a large board with the carrot and cucumber matchsticks. Sprinkle the vegetables with salt and set aside for 15 minutes.

2 In a bowl, mix together the chillies and onion rings, and add the sliced gherkins and ground peanuts. Tip the salted vegetables into a colander, rinse well with cold water and pat dry with kitchen paper.

3 Put the vegetables into a salad bowl and add the chilli mixture and cooked chicken. In a small bowl, mix the gherkin liquid with the garlic, sugar and vinegar. Pour over the salad and toss lightly, then serve immediately.

> **Cook's Tip**
> *Add a little more cider or white wine vinegar to the dressing if a sharper taste is preferred.*

Hot-and-sour Chicken Salad

Another salad from Vietnam, in which deliciously spiced chicken is served hot on crisp vegetables.

Serves 4–6

2 skinless chicken breast fillets
1 small fresh red chilli, seeded
    and finely chopped
1cm/1/2in piece fresh root ginger,
    peeled and finely chopped
1 garlic clove, crushed
15ml/1 tbsp crunchy
    peanut butter
30ml/2 tbsp chopped fresh
    coriander (cilantro)
5ml/1 tsp sugar
2.5ml/1/2 tsp salt
15ml/1 tbsp rice or white
    wine vinegar
60ml/4 tbsp vegetable oil
10ml/2 tsp fish sauce (optional)
115g/4oz/ 1/2 cup beansprouts
1 head Chinese leaves (Chinese
    cabbage), roughly shredded
2 medium carrots, cut
    into matchsticks
1 red onion, cut into thin rings
2 large pickled gherkins, sliced

1 Slice the chicken thinly, place in a shallow bowl and set aside.

2 Grind the chilli, ginger and garlic in a mortar with a pestle. Add the peanut butter, coriander, sugar and salt. Add the vinegar, 30ml/2 tbsp of the oil and the fish sauce, if using. Combine well.

3 Cover the chicken with the spice mixture and leave to marinate for at least 2–3 hours.

4 Heat the remaining oil in a wok or frying pan. Add the chicken and cook for 10–12 minutes, tossing occasionally.

5 Arrange the beansprouts, Chinese leaves, carrots, onion and gherkins on a serving platter or individual plates and place the slices of chicken on top. Pour over the pan juices and serve immediately.

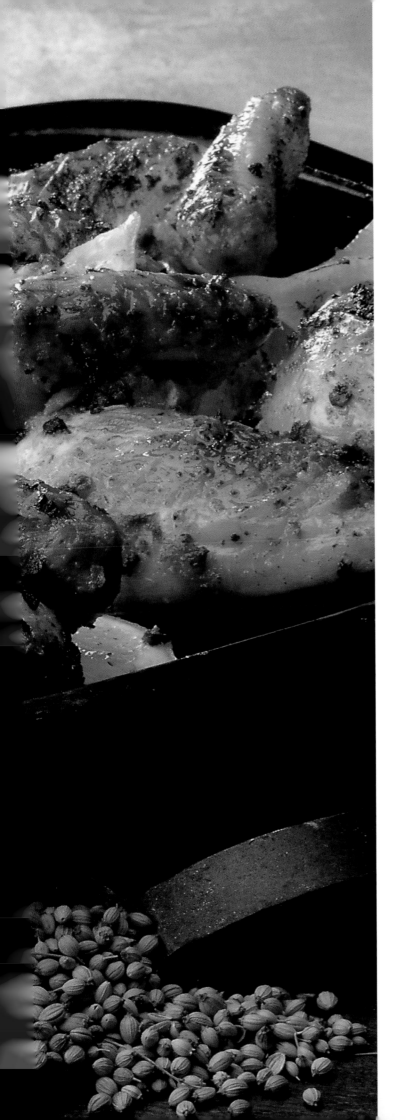

GRILLS, STIR-FRIES & SAUTÉS

Whether drumsticks, thighs, breast portions or quarters, chicken is the ideal choice for these quick-cooking methods and is perfect for the barbecue. Livening up otherwise rather bland and unexciting grills and sautés is universally popular, but every country has its own special way of combining spices and adding unique flavours. Of course, chillies – fresh and dried – feature in many recipes, but the fragrant dishes of Thailand, for example, are quite different from the more robust ones of Italy. Cajun, Caribbean, Indian and Chinese spice mixes are instantly identifiable to lovers of well-seasoned and piquant food.

The recipes in this chapter have been inspired by dishes from around the world. It not only features fiery favourites, such as jerk chicken, and chicken satay, but also offers some less familiar, but no less tongue-tingling recipes to add zing to your repertoire. Try Cajun-spiced Chicken from the deep South, Grilled Cashew Nut Chicken from Bali or Mexican Grilled Chicken with Pica de Gallo Salsa. In their different ways, marinades, coatings, pastes and sauces are used to pep up the flavour of chicken and, at the same time, keep it moist and tender when exposed to the fierce heat of the grill (broiler), barbecue, wok or frying pan.

Tandoori Chicken Kebabs

Before it is cooked, the chicken is marinated in a mixture of yogurt and lemon juice, flavoured with tandoori paste, garlic and fresh coriander.

Serves 4
4 skinless chicken breast fillets, about 175g/6oz each
15ml/1 tbsp lemon juice
45ml/3 tbsp tandoori paste
45ml/3 tbsp natural (plain) yogurt
1 garlic clove, crushed
30ml/2 tbsp chopped fresh coriander (cilantro)
1 small onion, cut into wedges and separated into layers
a little oil, for brushing
salt and freshly ground black pepper
fresh coriander (cilantro) sprigs, to garnish
pilau rice and naan bread, to serve

1 Cut the chicken fillets into 2.5cm/1in cubes, place in a bowl and add the lemon juice, tandoori paste, yogurt, garlic, coriander and seasoning. Cover and leave to marinate in the refrigerator for 2–3 hours.

2 Preheat the grill (broiler) to high. Thread alternate pieces of marinated chicken and onion on to 4 skewers.

3 Brush the onions with a little oil, lay on a grill (broiling) rack and cook under the grill for 10–12 minutes, turning once to ensure even cooking.

4 Garnish the kebabs with fresh coriander and serve immediately with pilau rice and naan bread.

Cook's Tip
Use chopped, boned and skinned chicken thighs, or turkey breast portions, for a cheaper alternative. Tandoori paste is available from Indian foodstores and many supermarkets.

Devilled Chicken

This hot and spicy chicken barbecue dish is a speciality of the Abruzzo region of Italy and uses a piquant marinade of dried red chillies.

Serves 4
120ml/4fl oz/ ½ cup olive oil
finely grated rind and juice of 1 large lemon
2 garlic cloves, finely chopped
10ml/2 tsp finely chopped or crumbled dried red chillies
12 skinless, boneless chicken thighs, each cut into 3 or 4 pieces
salt and freshly ground black pepper
flat leaf parsley, to garnish
lemon wedges and green salad, to serve

1 Make a marinade by mixing the oil, lemon rind and juice, garlic and chillies in a large, shallow non-metallic dish. Add salt and pepper to taste, and whisk well.

2 Add the chicken pieces to the dish, turning to coat with the marinade. Cover and place in the refrigerator for at least 4 hours, or preferably overnight.

3 When ready to cook, prepare a barbecue or preheat the grill (broiler) and thread the chicken pieces on to 8 oiled metal skewers. Barbecue (grill) over hot coals or cook under a hot grill (broiler) for 6–8 minutes, turning frequently, until tender.

4 Serve hot, garnished with flat leaf parsley and accompanied by lemon wedges for squeezing and a green salad.

Cook's Tip
Thread the chicken pieces zig-zag fashion on to the skewers so that they do not fall off during cooking.

Chicken Satay with Peanut Sauce

Marinated chicken kebabs served with a peanut sauce.

Serves 4–6
4 chicken breast fillets
15ml/1 tbsp coriander seeds
10ml/2 tsp fennel seeds
2 garlic cloves, crushed
5cm/2in piece lemon
   grass, shredded
2.5ml/½ tsp ground turmeric
10ml/2 tsp sugar
2.5ml/½ tsp salt
30ml/2 tbsp soy sauce
15ml/1 tbsp sesame oil
juice of ½ lime

mint leaves, lime wedges and
   cucumber batons, to garnish
lettuce, to serve

For the peanut sauce
150g/5oz/1¼ cups raw peanuts
15ml/1 tbsp vegetable oil,
   plus extra
2 shallots, finely chopped
1 garlic clove, crushed
1–2 small fresh chillies, seeded
   and finely chopped
1cm/½ in cube shrimp paste
30ml/2 tbsp tamarind sauce
120ml/4fl oz/½ cup coconut milk
15ml/1 tbsp clear honey

1 Cut the chicken into thin strips and thread, zig-zag fashion, on to 12 bamboo skewers. Arrange on a flat plate and set aside.

2 Dry-fry the coriander and fennel seeds in a wok. Grind with a pestle and mortar or food processor, then return to the wok and add the garlic, lemon grass, turmeric, sugar, salt, soy sauce, sesame oil and lime juice. Allow the mixture to cool. Spread it over the chicken and leave in a cool place for up to 8 hours.

3 For the sauce, stir-fry the peanuts with a little oil. Turn out on to a cloth and rub with your hands to remove the skins. Process in a food processor for 2 minutes. Heat the oil in a wok and fry the shallots, garlic and chillies until softened. Add the shrimp paste, tamarind sauce, coconut milk and honey. Simmer briefly, add to the peanuts and process to a thick sauce. Pour into a serving bowl.

4 Brush the chicken with a little vegetable oil and cook under a preheated grill (broiler) for 6–8 minutes. Serve on a bed of lettuce, garnished with mint leaves, lime wedges and cucumber batons and accompanied by the peanut sauce.

Chicken Tikka Masala

Tender chicken pieces cooked in a creamy, spicy sauce with a hint of tomato and served on naan bread.

Serves 4
675g/1½ lb skinless chicken
   breast fillets
90ml/6 tbsp tikka paste
60ml/4 tbsp natural (plain) yogurt
30ml/2 tbsp oil
1 onion, chopped
1 garlic clove, crushed
1 fresh green chilli, seeded
   and chopped

2.5cm/1in piece fresh root
   ginger, grated
15ml/1 tbsp tomato
   purée (paste)
15ml/1 tbsp ground almonds
250ml/8fl oz/1 cup water
45ml/3 tbsp butter, melted
50ml/2fl oz/¼ cup double
   (heavy) cream
15ml/1 tbsp lemon juice
fresh coriander (cilantro) sprigs,
   natural (plain) yogurt and
   toasted cumin seeds,
   to garnish
naan bread, to serve

1 Cut the chicken into 2.5cm/1in cubes. Put 45ml/3 tbsp of the tikka paste and all of the yogurt into a bowl. Add the chicken, turn to coat well and leave to marinate for 20 minutes.

2 For the tikka sauce, heat the oil in a pan and fry the onion, garlic, chilli and ginger for 5 minutes. Add the remaining tikka paste and fry for 2 minutes. Add the tomato purée, ground almonds and water, and simmer for 15 minutes.

3 Meanwhile, thread the chicken on to wooden kebab skewers. Preheat the grill (broiler).

4 Brush the chicken with the melted butter and grill (broil) under a medium heat for 15 minutes, turning occasionally.

5 Put the tikka sauce into a food processor or blender and process until smooth. Return to the pan and stir in the cream and lemon juice.

6 Remove the chicken from the skewers and add to the tikka sauce. Simmer for 5 minutes. Serve on naan bread and garnish with coriander, yogurt and toasted cumin seeds.

Blackened Cajun Chicken & Corn

A classic method of cooking poultry in a spiced coating, from the deep South of the United States. Traditionally, the coating should begin to char and blacken slightly at the edges.

Serves 4

8 chicken joints, e.g. drumsticks,
  thighs or wings
2 whole sweetcorn cobs
10ml/2 tsp garlic salt
10ml/2 tsp freshly ground
  black pepper
7.5ml/1 ½ tsp ground cumin
7.5ml/1 ½ tsp paprika
5ml/1 tsp cayenne pepper
45ml/3 tbsp melted butter
chopped fresh parsley, to garnish

1 Cut any excess fat from the chicken, but leave the skin on. Slash the deepest parts with a knife to allow the flavours to penetrate the flesh.

2 Pull the husks and silks off the corn cobs and discard. Cut the cobs into thick slices.

3 In a small bowl, mix together all the spices. Put the chicken and corn in a large bowl and brush with melted butter. Sprinkle the spices over them and toss well to coat evenly.

4 Cook the chicken pieces on a medium-hot barbecue or under a preheated grill (broiler) for about 25 minutes, turning occasionally. Add the corn after 15 minutes of the cooking time and cook, turning often, until golden brown. Serve hot, garnished with chopped parsley.

> **Cook's Tip**
> The natural sugar which gives sweetcorn its characteristic flavour starts to turn to starch immediately after picking. When buying, look for plump kernels and always use the cobs on the day of purchase.

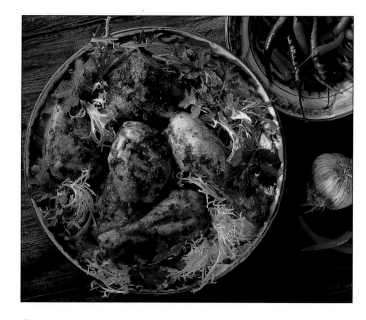

Barbecued Jerk Chicken

Jerk refers to the blend of herb and spice seasoning rubbed into meat before it is roasted over charcoal, usually sprinkled with pimiento berries, to make this tasty Caribbean dish.

Serves 4

8 chicken portions
oil, for brushing
salt and freshly ground
  black pepper
salad leaves, to serve

For the marinade

5ml/1 tsp ground allspice
5ml/1 tsp ground cinnamon
5ml/1 tsp dried thyme
1.5ml/ ¼ tsp grated nutmeg
10ml/2 tsp demerara (raw) sugar
2 garlic cloves, crushed
15ml/1 tbsp finely chopped onion
15ml/1 tbsp chopped spring
  onion (scallion)
15ml/1 tbsp vinegar
30ml/2 tbsp oil
15ml/1 tbsp lime juice
1 hot fresh chilli, chopped

1 To make the marinade, combine all the ingredients in a small bowl and mash them together well to form a thick paste.

2 Lay the chicken portions on a plate or board and make several lengthways slits in the flesh. Rub the seasoning all over the chicken and into the slits. Place the chicken portions in a dish, cover with clear film (plastic wrap) and marinate for several hours, or preferably overnight, in the refrigerator.

3 Preheat the grill (broiler) or prepare the barbecue. Shake off any excess seasoning from the chicken. Brush with oil and place either on a baking sheet or on a barbecue. Cook under the grill (broiler) for 45 minutes, turning often, or barbecue (grill) over hot coals for 30 minutes, turning often. Serve immediately with salad leaves.

> **Cook's Tip**
> The flavour is best if you marinate the chicken overnight. Sprinkle the charcoal with aromatic herbs, such as bay leaves, for even more flavour when cooking.

Spicy Barbecued Chicken

A very easy dish that can be cooked either on the barbecue or in the oven. The sauce has all the hot, sharp and sweet flavours that you would expect.

Serves 4

45ml/3 tbsp vegetable oil
1 large onion, chopped
175ml/6fl oz/ ¾ cup
    tomato ketchup
175ml/6fl oz/ ¾ cup water
40ml/2½ tbsp fresh lemon juice
25ml/1½ tbsp grated horseradish
15ml/1 tbsp light brown sugar
15ml/1 tbsp French mustard
1.3kg/3lb chicken portions
cooked rice, to serve

1 Preheat the oven, if using, to 180°C/350°F/Gas 4. Heat 15ml/1 tbsp of the oil in a pan. Add the onion and cook for about 5 minutes until softened. Stir in the tomato ketchup, water, lemon juice, horseradish, sugar and mustard, and bring to the boil. Reduce the heat and simmer the sauce for 10 minutes, stirring occasionally.

2 Meanwhile, heat the remaining oil in a heavy frying pan. Add the chicken portions and brown on all sides. Remove from the pan and drain on kitchen paper.

3 Place the chicken in a 28 x 23cm/11 x 9in ovenproof dish and pour the sauce over the top.

4 Bake in the oven for about 1¼ hours until the chicken is cooked and tender, basting occasionally. Alternatively, cook on a barbecue over a medium heat for 40–50 minutes, turning once and brushing frequently with the sauce. Serve the chicken on a bed of cooked rice.

> **Cook's Tip**
> *For a hotter flavour, use English (hot) mustard.*

Barbecued Chicken Thai-style

Barbecued chicken is served almost everywhere in Thailand, from portable roadside stalls to sports stadiums and beaches.

Serves 4–6

1.5kg/3½ lb chicken, cut into
    8–10 pieces
lime wedges and finely sliced red
    chillies, to garnish
cooked rice, to serve

For the marinade
2 lemon grass stalks, chopped
2.5cm/1in piece fresh root ginger
6 garlic cloves
4 shallots
½ bunch fresh coriander
    (cilantro) roots
15ml/1 tbsp palm sugar
120ml/4fl oz/ ½ cup
    coconut milk
30ml/2 tbsp Thai fish sauce
30ml/2 tbsp soy sauce

1 To make the marinade, put all the ingredients into a food processor and process until smooth.

2 Put the chicken pieces in a wide, shallow dish and pour over the marinade. Leave to marinate in the refrigerator for at least 4 hours or overnight.

3 Prepare the barbecue or preheat the oven to 200°C/400°F/Gas 6. Cook the chicken pieces over glowing coals, or place on a rack over a roasting pan and bake in the oven for about 20–30 minutes or until the chicken is cooked and golden brown. Turn the pieces occasionally and brush frequently with the marinade.

4 Garnish with lime wedges and finely sliced red chillies, and serve with rice.

> **Cook's Tip**
> *Made from salted anchovies, Thai fish sauce – also known as nam pla – is widely used in Thai cooking in much the same way as soy sauce is used in Chinese cuisine. It is strongly flavoured and very salty, so use with caution. It is available from Asian foodstores and many supermarkets.*

Thai Grilled Chicken

Thai grilled chicken is especially delicious when cooked on the barbecue. It should be served with a dipping sauce.

Serves 4–6
900g/2lb chicken drumsticks
  or thighs
5ml/1 tsp whole
  black peppercorns
2.5ml/ ½ tsp caraway or
  cumin seeds
20ml/4 tsp sugar
10ml/2 tsp paprika

2cm/ ¾in piece fresh root
  ginger, peeled
3 garlic cloves, crushed
15g/ ½ oz fresh coriander
  (cilantro), white root or stem,
  finely chopped
45ml/3 tbsp vegetable oil
salt
6–8 lettuce leaves, to serve

For the garnish
½ cucumber, cut into strips
4 spring onions
  (scallions), trimmed
2 limes, quartered

1 Chop through the narrow end of each chicken drumstick with a heavy knife. Score the chicken pieces deeply to allow the marinade to penetrate. Set aside in a shallow bowl.

2 Grind the peppercorns, caraway or cumin seeds and sugar using a pestle and mortar or food processor. Add the paprika, ginger, garlic, coriander and oil, and grind to a paste. Spread the marinade over the chicken and place in the refrigerator for 6 hours.

3 Preheat the grill (broiler) or prepare the barbecue. Cook the chicken for 20 minutes, turning once. Season with salt to taste. Serve on a bed of lettuce leaves, garnished with cucumber, spring onions and lime quarters.

> **Cook's Tip**
> *Spices are more flavoursome when freshly ground rather than bought ready ground. You can use a pestle and mortar or a small coffee mill kept especially for this purpose. Custom-made spice grinders are also available.*

Grilled Spiced Chicken

The sharpness of fresh lime balances the heat and strength of the spices.

Serves 4
5ml/1 tsp coriander seeds
5ml/1 tsp cumin seeds
2 limes
2 garlic cloves, crushed

60ml/4 tbsp chopped
  fresh coriander (cilantro)
1 small fresh green chilli, seeded
  and finely chopped
30ml/2 tbsp light soy sauce
60ml/4 tbsp sunflower oil
4 skinless chicken breast fillets,
  about 175g/6oz each
green vegetables, to serve

1 Crush the coriander and cumin seeds using a pestle and mortar or a spice grinder. Cut the rind from the limes into thin shreds using a zester. Squeeze the juice. Blend the spices, lime rind and juice, garlic, fresh coriander, chilli, soy sauce and oil in a bowl. Add the chicken, turn to coat thoroughly, then cover and marinate in the refrigerator for 24 hours.

2 Remove the chicken from the marinade. Heat a grill (broiler) or griddle pan and cook the chicken for about 4–6 minutes on each side or until cooked through. Serve with green vegetables.

Thai Dipping Sauce

This has a fiery strength, so use with caution.

Makes 120ml/4fl oz/½ cup
15ml/1 tbsp vegetable oil
15ml/1 tbsp Thai fish sauce
2 garlic cloves, finely chopped
2cm/¾in piece root ginger,
  peeled and finely chopped
3 fresh red chillies, chopped
15ml/1 tbsp finely chopped
  fresh coriander
  (cilantro) root

20ml/4 tsp sugar
45ml/3 tbsp dark soy sauce
juice of ½ lime

1 Heat the oil, fish sauce, garlic, ginger and chillies for 1–2 minutes.
2 Remove from the heat and add the remaining ingredients.

Indonesian Chicken Grill

The flavour of this dish will be more intense if the chicken is marinated for several hours or overnight.

Serves 4
1.5kg/3½ lb chicken
4 garlic cloves, crushed
2 lemon grass stalks, lower 5cm/2in sliced
1cm/½in fresh galangal, peeled and sliced
5ml/1 tsp ground turmeric
about 475ml/16fl oz/2 cups water
3–4 bay leaves
45ml/3 tbsp each dark and light soy sauce
50g/2oz butter or margarine
salt
fresh coriander (cilantro), to garnish
boiled rice, to serve

1 Cut the chicken into 4 or 8 portions. Slash the fleshy part of each portion twice and set aside.

2 Put the garlic, lemon grass, galangal, turmeric and salt into a food processor and process to a paste or grind using a pestle and mortar. Rub the paste into the chicken pieces and leave for at least 30 minutes. Wear rubber gloves for this, as the turmeric will stain heavily; or wash your hands immediately after using.

3 Transfer the chicken pieces to a wok or heavy pan and pour in the water. Add the bay leaves and bring to the boil. Cover and cook gently for 30 minutes, adding a little more water if necessary. Stir from time to time.

4 Preheat the grill (broiler) or barbecue, or preheat the oven to 200°C/400°F/Gas 6. Just before transferring the chicken, add the two soy sauces to the pan along with the butter or margarine. Cook until the chicken is well coated and the sauce has almost been absorbed.

5 Transfer to the grill, barbecue or oven and cook for a further 10–15 minutes, turning the pieces often so that they become golden brown all over. Take care not to let them burn. Baste with the remaining sauce during cooking. Serve with boiled rice, garnished with coriander leaves.

Grilled Cashew Nut Chicken

This dish comes from Bali where nuts are widely used as a base for sauces and marinades. Serve with a green salad and hot chilli dipping sauce.

Serves 4–6
4 chicken legs
sliced radishes and sliced cucumber, to garnish
Chinese leaves (Chinese cabbage) and chilli dipping sauce, to serve

For the marinade
50g/2oz/½ cup raw cashew or macadamia nuts
2 shallots or 1 small onion, finely chopped
2 garlic cloves, crushed
2 small fresh red chillies, chopped
5cm/2in piece lemon grass
15ml/1 tbsp tamarind sauce
30ml/2 tbsp dark soy sauce
15ml/1 tbsp fish sauce (optional)
10ml/2 tsp sugar
2.5ml/½ tsp salt
15ml/1 tbsp rice or white wine vinegar

1 Using a sharp knife, slash the chicken legs several times through to the bone and chop off the knuckle end. Place the chicken in a wide, shallow dish and set aside.

2 To make the marinade, grind the cashew or macadamia nuts in a food processor or using a pestle and mortar.

3 Add the shallots or onion, garlic, chillies and lemon grass, and blend. Add the remaining marinade ingredients.

4 Spread the marinade over the chicken and leave in the refrigerator for up to 8 hours.

5 Preheat the grill (broiler) or prepare the barbecue. Grill (broil) the chicken under a moderate heat or cook on the barbecue for 15 minutes on each side. Transfer to a serving dish lined with Chinese leaves, garnish with the radishes and cucumber, and serve, accompanied by chilli dipping sauce.

Chicken Breast Fillets Cooked in Spices & Coconut

The chicken is marinated in a highly aromatic, spicy coconut mixture.

Serves 4
200g/7oz block creamed coconut
  (coconut cream)
300ml/ ½ pint/1 ¼ cups
  boiling water
3 garlic cloves, chopped
2 spring onions
  (scallions), chopped
1 fresh green chilli, chopped
5cm/2in piece fresh root ginger,
  peeled and chopped

5ml/1 tsp fennel seeds
2.5ml/ ½ tsp black peppercorns
seeds from 4 cardamom pods
30ml/2 tbsp ground coriander
5ml/1 tsp ground cumin
5ml/1 tsp ground star anise
5ml/1 tsp grated nutmeg
2.5ml/ ½ tsp ground cloves
2.5ml/ ½ tsp ground turmeric
4 large skinless chicken
  breast fillets
onion rings and fresh coriander
  (cilantro) sprigs, to garnish
naan bread, to serve

1 Break up the coconut and put it in a jug (pitcher). Pour the boiling water over and set aside until completely dissolved. Place the garlic, spring onions, chilli, ginger and all the spices in a blender or food processor. Add the coconut mixture and process to a smooth paste.

2 Make several diagonal cuts across the chicken fillets. Arrange them in one layer in a shallow dish. Spoon over half the coconut mixture and toss well to coat the chicken evenly. Cover the dish and leave to marinate in the refrigerator for about 30 minutes, or overnight.

3 Cook the chicken under a preheated grill (broiler) or on a moderately hot barbecue for 12–15 minutes, turning once, until well browned and thoroughly cooked.

4 Heat the remaining coconut mixture gently until boiling. Serve with the chicken, garnished with onion rings and sprigs of coriander, and accompanied by naan bread.

Drumsticks with Devilish Sauce

Chicken drumsticks marinated with spices, coated with a hot, tomato-based sauce and served on a bed of yellow rice.

Serves 4
8 large chicken drumsticks

For the dry marinade
10ml/2 tsp salt
10ml/2 tsp caster
  (superfine) sugar
5ml/1 tsp freshly ground
  black pepper
5ml/1 tsp ground ginger
5ml/1 tsp paprika

5ml/1 tsp English (hot)
  mustard powder
30ml/2 tbsp olive oil

For the sauce
30ml/2 tbsp tomato ketchup
15ml/1 tbsp mushroom ketchup
15ml/1 tbsp chilli sauce
15ml/1 tbsp soy sauce
15ml/1 tbsp fruit sauce

For the yellow rice
25g/1oz/2 tbsp butter
1 medium onion, finely chopped
5ml/1 tsp ground turmeric
225g/8oz/generous 1 cup
  cooked rice

1 To make the dry marinade, combine all the ingredients in a bowl. Place the chicken drumsticks in a wide, shallow dish. Rub the marinade into the drumsticks, cover with clear film (plastic wrap) and leave for at least 1 hour, or preferably overnight.

2 Preheat the grill (broiler). Lay the drumsticks on a grill (broiling) rack and grill (broil) slowly under a medium heat for 10 minutes, turning occasionally, until brown and crisp.

3 Meanwhile, to make the sauce, mix all the ingredients together and spoon over the chicken. Continue to cook the chicken for a further 5–7 minutes, basting frequently.

4 To make the yellow rice, heat the butter in a large pan, add the onion and cook until tender. Add the turmeric and cook for a further minute.

5 Add the cooked rice and stir to reheat and colour. Spoon on to a serving plate and arrange the devilled drumsticks on top. Serve immediately.

Grilled Chicken with Pica de Gallo Salsa

This dish originates from Mexico. Its hot, fruity flavours form the essence of Tex-Mex cooking.

Serves 4
4 chicken breast portions
pinch each of celery salt and
    cayenne pepper, combined
30ml/2 tbsp vegetable oil
fresh coriander (cilantro) sprigs,
    to garnish
corn chips, to serve

For the salsa
275g/10 oz watermelon
175g/6oz canteloupe melon
1 small red onion
1–2 fresh green chillies
30ml/2 tbsp lime juice
60ml/4 tbsp chopped
    fresh coriander (cilantro)
salt

1 Preheat a moderate grill (broiler). Slash the chicken breast portions deeply in several places. Season the chicken with celery salt and cayenne, brush with oil and grill (broil) for about 15 minutes, turning occasionally.

2 To make the salsa, remove the rind and as many seeds as you can from the melons. Finely dice the flesh and put it into a bowl. Finely chop the onion. Split the chillies (discarding the seeds if you do not want a very hot salsa) and chop. Mix the onion and chillies with the melon. Add the lime juice and chopped coriander, and season with a pinch of salt. Turn the salsa into a small bowl.

3 Arrange the grilled (broiled) chicken on a plate, and serve with the salsa and a handful of corn chips. Garnish with coriander sprigs.

Cook's Tip
To capture the spirit of Tex-Mex food, cook the chicken over a barbecue and eat shaded from the hot summer sun.

Spiced Barbecued Poussins

The coating of ground cumin and coriander on the poussins keeps them moist while they are cooking as well as giving them a delicious spicy flavour.

Serves 4
2 garlic cloves, roughly chopped
5ml/1 tsp ground cumin
5ml/1 tsp ground coriander
pinch of cayenne pepper
1/2 small onion, chopped
60ml/4 tbsp olive oil
2.5ml/ 1/2 tsp salt
2 poussins
lemon wedges, to garnish

1 Combine the garlic, cumin, coriander, cayenne pepper, onion, olive oil and salt in a blender or food processor. Process to make a paste that will spread smoothly.

2 Cut the poussins in half lengthways. Place them skin-side up in a shallow dish and spread with the spice paste. Cover and leave to marinate in a cool place for 2 hours.

3 Barbecue (grill) or grill (broil) the poussins for about 15–20 minutes, turning frequently, until cooked and lightly charred on the outside. Serve garnished with lemon wedges.

Cook's Tip
Quail can also be cooked in this way. Quail are quite small birds, weighing 115–150g/4–5oz, but with a surprising amount of meat. One bird will usually make a substantial single portion. The meat has quite a delicate flavour and can dry out easily, so this is an especially good way of cooking quail. Wild quail is no longer available, but fresh or frozen Japanese quail is widely available from many supermarkets.

Cashew Chicken

In this Chinese-inspired dish, tender pieces of chicken are stir-fried with cashews, red chillies and a touch of garlic for a delicious combination.

Serves 4–6
450g/1lb chicken breast fillets
30ml/2 tbsp vegetable oil
2 garlic cloves, sliced
4 dried red chillies, chopped
1 red (bell) pepper, seeded and
  cut into 2cm/¾in dice
30ml/2 tbsp oyster sauce
15ml/1 tbsp soy sauce
pinch of sugar
1 bunch spring onions (scallions),
  cut into 5cm/2in lengths
175g/6oz/1½ cups cashew
  nuts, roasted
fresh coriander (cilantro) leaves,
  to garnish

1 Remove and discard the skin from the chicken. Using a sharp knife, cut the chicken into bite-size pieces. Set aside.

2 Heat the oil in a wok and swirl it around. Add the garlic and dried chillies, and fry until golden.

3 Add the chicken and stir-fry until it changes colour, then add the red pepper. If necessary, add a little water.

4 Stir in the oyster sauce, soy sauce and sugar. Add the spring onions and cashews. Stir-fry for 1–2 minutes. Serve, garnished with fresh coriander leaves.

Variations
For an extra-spicy dish, season with cayenne pepper to taste just before serving. For a slightly different flavour, substitute halved walnuts for the cashews. For a more substantial dish, add 150g/5oz/2 cups sliced mushrooms and 150g/5oz mangetouts (snow peas) with the red pepper in step 3.

Stir-fried Chicken with Basil & Chillies

Deep-frying the basil adds another dimension to this easy Thai dish. Thai basil, which is sometimes known as Holy basil, has a unique, pungent flavour that is both spicy and sharp. The dull leaves have serrated edges.

Serves 4–6
45ml/3 tbsp vegetable oil
4 garlic cloves, sliced
2–4 fresh red chillies, seeded
  and chopped
450g/1lb boneless chicken
30–45ml/2–3 tbsp Thai fish sauce
10ml/2 tsp dark soy sauce
5ml/1 tsp sugar
10–12 Thai basil leaves

For the garnish
2 fresh red chillies, finely sliced
20 Thai basil leaves, deep-
  fried (optional)

1 Heat the oil in a wok or large frying pan and swirl it around. Add the garlic and chillies, and stir-fry until golden.

2 Cut the chicken into bitesize pieces, add to the wok or pan and stir-fry until it changes colour.

3 Season with fish sauce, soy sauce and sugar. Continue to stir-fry for 3–4 minutes or until the chicken is cooked.

4 Stir in the fresh Thai basil leaves. Garnish with sliced chillies and the deep-fried basil, if using.

Cook's Tip
To deep-fry Thai basil leaves, make sure that the leaves are completely dry. Deep-fry in hot oil for about 30–40 seconds, lift out and drain on kitchen paper.

Chicken Stir-fry with Five Spices

The chicken is marinated in an aromatic blend of spices and stir-fried with crisp vegetables. If you find it too spicy, serve with a spoonful of sour cream or yogurt.

Serves 4

2.5ml/ ½ tsp each ground
   turmeric and ground ginger
5ml/1 tsp each salt and freshly
   ground black pepper
10ml/2 tsp ground cumin
15ml/1 tbsp ground coriander
15ml/1 tbsp caster
   (superfine) sugar
450g/1lb skinless chicken
   breast fillets
1 bunch spring onions (scallions)
4 celery sticks
2 red (bell) peppers, seeded
1 yellow (bell) pepper, seeded
175g/6oz courgettes (zucchini)
175g/6oz mangetouts (snow
   peas) or sugar snap peas
about 45ml/3 tbsp sunflower oil
15ml/1 tbsp lime juice
15ml/1 tbsp clear honey

1 Mix together the turmeric, ginger, salt, pepper, cumin, coriander and sugar in a bowl until well combined. Cut the chicken into bitesize strips. Add to the spice mixture and stir to coat the chicken pieces thoroughly. Set aside.

2 Prepare the vegetables. Cut the spring onions, celery and peppers into 5cm/2in long, thin strips. Cut the courgettes at a slight angle into thin rounds, and trim the mangetouts or sugar snap peas.

3 Heat 30ml/2 tbsp oil in a large, heavy frying pan or wok. Stir-fry the chicken, in batches, until cooked through and golden brown, adding a little more oil if necessary. Remove the chicken from the pan and keep warm.

4 Add a little more oil to the pan and cook the spring onions, celery, peppers and courgettes over a medium heat for about 8–10 minutes until beginning to soften and turn golden. Add the mangetouts or sugar snap peas and cook for a further 2 minutes.

5 Return the chicken to the pan, with the lime juice and honey. Cook for 2 minutes. Adjust the seasoning and serve.

Spiced Chicken Sauté

A rich tomato sauce coats this chicken, which is first oven-cooked or fried.

Serves 4

1.5kg/3½ lb chicken, cut into
   8 pieces
5ml/1 tsp each salt and freshly
   ground black pepper
2 garlic cloves, crushed
sunflower oil
sliced fresh red chilli and
   deep-fried onions, to
   garnish (optional)
boiled rice, to serve

For the sauce

25g/1oz/2 tbsp butter
30ml/2 tbsp sunflower oil
1 onion, sliced
4 garlic cloves, crushed
2 large ripe beefsteak tomatoes,
   chopped, or 400g/14oz can
   chopped tomatoes with
   chilli, drained
600ml/1 pint/2½ cups water
50ml/2fl oz/ ¼ cup dark
   soy sauce
salt and freshly ground
   black pepper

1 Preheat the oven to 190°C/375°F/Gas 5. Make 2 slashes in the fleshy part of each chicken piece. Rub well with the salt, pepper and garlic. Drizzle with a little oil and bake for 30 minutes until brown. Alternatively, shallow fry in hot oil for 12–15 minutes.

2 To make the sauce, heat the butter and oil in a wok or frying pan, and fry the onion and garlic until soft. Add the tomatoes, water, soy sauce and seasoning. Boil briskly for 5 minutes to reduce the sauce and concentrate the flavour.

3 Add the chicken to the sauce in the wok. Turn the chicken pieces over in the sauce to coat them well. Continue cooking slowly for about 20 minutes until the chicken pieces are tender. Stir the mixture occasionally.

4 Arrange the chicken on a warmed serving platter and garnish with the sliced chilli and deep-fried onions, if using. Serve with boiled rice.

Deep-fried Onions

A traditional garnish and accompaniment to many Indonesian dishes. Asian stores sell them ready-prepared, but it is simple to make them at home.

Makes 450g/1lb

450g/1lb onions
oil, for deep-frying

1 Peel the onions and slice as evenly and thinly as possible. Spread out on kitchen paper, in an airy place, and set aside to dry for 30 minutes to 2 hours.

2 Heat the oil in a deep-fat fryer or wok to 190°C/375°F and fry the onions, in batches, until crisp and golden, turning constantly. Drain well on kitchen paper and allow to cool. Store in an airtight container for 2–3 days.

Spiced Honey Chicken Wings

Be prepared to get very sticky when you eat these wings, as the best way to enjoy them is by eating them with your fingers. Provide individual finger bowls for your guests.

Serves 4

1 fresh red chilli, finely chopped
5ml/1 tsp chilli powder
5ml/1 tsp ground ginger
rind of 1 lime, finely grated
12 chicken wings
60ml/4 tbsp sunflower oil
15ml/1 tbsp chopped
   fresh coriander (cilantro)
30ml/2 tbsp soy sauce
50ml/3½ tbsp clear honey

1 Mix the fresh chilli, chilli powder, ground ginger and lime rind together in a small bowl. Place the chicken wings in a wide, shallow dish. Rub the spice mixture into the chicken skins and leave for at least 2 hours to allow the flavours to penetrate.

2 Heat a wok or heavy frying pan and add half the oil. When the oil is hot, add half the wings and stir-fry for 10 minutes, turning regularly until crisp and golden. Drain on kitchen paper. Repeat with the remaining oil and wings.

3 Add the coriander to the hot wok and stir-fry for 30 seconds, then return the wings to the wok and stir-fry for 1 minute.

4 Stir in the soy sauce and clear honey and stir-fry for another minute. Serve the chicken wings hot, with the sauce drizzled over them.

> **Cook's Tip**
> *These wings are perfect party food, as they are inexpensive, take little time to cook and are easy to nibble. For a more filling meal, use the same flavourings for chicken drumsticks, but cook under the grill (broiler) for 12–15 minutes, turning frequently, until cooked through and golden.*

Cajun-spiced Chicken

These chicken breast fillets are seared in a very hot frying pan which, for best results, should be of heavy cast iron and well seasoned.

Serves 6

6 medium skinless chicken
   breast fillets
75g/3oz/6 tbsp butter
   or margarine
5ml/1 tsp garlic powder
10ml/2 tsp onion powder
5ml/2 tsp cayenne pepper
10ml/2 tsp paprika
7.5ml/1½ tsp salt
2.5ml/½ tsp freshly ground
   white pepper
5ml/1 tsp freshly ground
   black pepper
1.5ml/¼ tsp ground cumin
5ml/1 tsp dried thyme
salad leaves and (bell) pepper
   strips, to garnish

1 Slice each chicken breast in half horizontally, making 2 pieces of about the same thickness. Flatten them slightly with the heel of your hand. Lay them on a large plate or place in a wide shallow dish.

2 Melt the butter or margarine in a small pan over a low heat without letting it colour.

3 Combine all the remaining ingredients, apart from the garnish, in a bowl and stir to blend well. Brush the chicken pieces on both sides with a little of the melted butter or margarine, then sprinkle evenly with the seasoning mixture.

4 Heat a large, heavy frying pan over a high heat for about 5–8 minutes, until a drop of water sprinkled on the surface sizzles.

5 Drizzle 5ml/1 tsp melted butter on to each chicken piece. Place them carefully in the frying pan in an even layer, 2–3 at a time, and cook for about 2–3 minutes, until the underside begins to blacken. Turn and cook the other side for 2–3 minutes more. Serve hot, garnished with salad leaves and pepper strips.

Caribbean Fried Chicken

This crispy chicken is superb hot or cold. Served with a salad or vegetables, it makes a delicious lunch and is ideal for picnics and snacks too.

Serves 4–6
4 chicken drumsticks
4 chicken thighs
10ml/2 tsp curry powder
2.5ml/ ½ tsp garlic granules
2.5ml/ ½ tsp freshly ground black pepper
2.5ml/ ½ tsp paprika
about 300ml/ ½ pint/ 1¼ cups milk
oil, for deep-frying
50g/2oz/ ½ cup plain (all-purpose) flour
salt
mixed salad, to serve

1 Place the chicken pieces in a large bowl and sprinkle with the curry powder, garlic granules, black pepper, paprika and salt to taste. Rub the spices well into the chicken, then cover and leave to marinate in a cool place for at least 2 hours, or overnight in the refrigerator.

2 Preheat the oven to 180°C/350°F/Gas 4. Pour enough milk into the bowl to cover the chicken and leave to stand for a further 15 minutes.

3 Heat the oil in a large, heavy pan or deep-fat fryer. Tip the flour on to a plate. Shake off excess milk from the chicken and dip each piece in the flour, turning it to coat well. Fry 2–3 pieces at a time until golden but not cooked. Continue until all the chicken pieces are fried.

4 Remove the chicken pieces from the oil using a slotted spoon and place on a baking sheet. Bake in the oven for about 30 minutes. Serve hot or cold with mixed salad.

> **Variation**
> *This recipe would work as well with turkey breast portions, but would require only 15–20 minutes cooking time in the oven.*

Spicy Fried Chicken

Chicken portions are soaked in buttermilk before they are coated with spiced flour and fried.

Serves 4
120ml/4fl oz/ ½ cup buttermilk
1.3kg/3lb chicken portions
vegetable oil, for frying
50g/2oz/ ½ cup plain (all-purpose) flour
15ml/1 tbsp paprika
1.5ml/ ¼ tsp pepper
15ml/1 tbsp water

1 Pour the buttermilk into a large bowl and add the chicken pieces. Stir to coat, then set aside for 5 minutes.

2 Heat 5mm/¼in depth of oil in a large frying pan over a medium-high heat. Do not let the oil overheat.

3 In a bowl or plastic bag, combine the flour, paprika and pepper. One by one, lift the chicken pieces out of the buttermilk and dip into the flour to coat well all over, shaking off any excess.

4 Add the chicken pieces to the hot oil and fry for about 10 minutes until lightly browned, turning them over halfway through the cooking time.

5 Reduce the heat to low and add the water to the frying pan. Cover and cook for 30 minutes, turning the pieces over at 10-minute intervals. Uncover the pan and continue cooking for about 15 minutes until the chicken is very tender and the coating is crisp, turning every 5 minutes. Serve hot.

> **Cook's Tip**
> *Buttermilk, available from supermarkets, is a by-product of the butter-making process. Nowadays, it is more often cultured skimmed milk produced under controlled conditions, which make it more stable.*

SPICY ROASTS, BAKES & CASSEROLES

This chapter is a real celebration of chicken's immense versatility. There seems to be no end to the number of ways in which it can be roasted, baked and casseroled – and no end to the spices that can liven up its flavour. Fruity and tangy, warming and aromatic, sweet and sour or devilishly hot, chicken – and the Sunday roast – will certainly never be boring again. A whole chicken can be flavoured with a hot-shot stuffing or smothered in a vibrant coating before roasting. Chicken portions can be combined with other positively pyrotechnic ingredients before baking or cooking in a casserole – ginger, sugar, lime juice and hot pepper sauce in Caribbean Ginger Chicken or chocolate and four different kinds of chillies in Mole Poblano de Guajolote, for example. Other recipes feature more classic, but no less piquant combinations, from chillies, lime juice and coriander (cilantro) to turmeric, lemon grass and coconut milk. Whether your favourite food is mild and Moroccan, tangy and Thai or incandescent and Indonesian, you are sure to find a recipe in this chapter that will fire your imagination.

Stuffed Roast Masala Chicken

At one time this dish was cooked only in Indian palaces.

Serves 4–6

1 sachet saffron powder
2.5ml/ ½ tsp freshly grated
   nutmeg
15ml/1 tbsp warm milk
1.3kg/3lb chicken
90ml/6 tbsp ghee
50g/2oz/ ½ cup desiccated (dry,
   unsweetened shredded)
   coconut, toasted
steamed carrots, to serve

For the stuffing

3 medium onions, finely chopped
2 fresh green chillies, chopped
50g/2oz/scant ½ cup sultanas
   (golden raisins)

50g/2oz/ ½ cup ground almonds
50g/2oz/ ½ cup dried apricots,
   soaked in water until soft
3 hard-boiled (hard-cooked) eggs,
   coarsely chopped
salt

For the masala

4 spring onions
   (scallions), chopped
2 garlic cloves, crushed
5ml/1 tsp Indian five-
   spice powder
4–6 green cardamom pods
2.5ml/ ½ tsp ground turmeric
5ml/1 tsp freshly ground
   black pepper
30ml/2 tbsp natural (plain) yogurt
75ml/5 tbsp hot water

1 Preheat the oven to 180°C/350°F/Gas 4. Mix the saffron, nutmeg and milk. Brush the inside of the chicken with the mixture and spread some under the skin. Heat 60ml/4 tbsp of the ghee in a frying pan and fry the chicken all over. Remove from the pan and keep warm.

2 To make the stuffing, fry the onions, chillies and sultanas for 2–3 minutes in the same pan. Cool, then mix in the almonds, apricots, eggs and salt, and stuff the chicken.

3 To make the masala, heat the remaining ghee in a pan and fry all the ingredients except the water for 2–3 minutes. Add to the water in a roasting pan.

4 Add the chicken and roast for 1 hour. Remove it and keep warm. Return the masala to the pan and cook to reduce. Pour over the chicken. Sprinkle with coconut and serve with carrots.

Roast Chicken with Almonds

In this Moroccan dish the chicken is stuffed with a mixture of couscous, nuts and fruit.

Serves 4

1.5kg/3½lb chicken
pinch of ground ginger
pinch of ground cinnamon
pinch of saffron, dissolved in
   30ml/2 tbsp boiling water
2 onions, chopped
300ml/ ½ pint/1¼ cups
   chicken stock
45ml/3 tbsp flaked
   (sliced) almonds
15ml/1 tbsp plain (all-
   purpose) flour
salt and freshly ground
   black pepper

lemon wedges and fresh coriander
(cilantro), to garnish

For the stuffing

50g/2oz/ ⅓ cup couscous
120ml/4fl oz/ ½ cup boiling
   chicken stock
20g/¾oz/1½ tbsp butter
1 shallot, finely chopped
½ small cooking apple, peeled,
   cored and chopped
25ml/5 tsp flaked
   (sliced) almonds
30ml/2 tbsp ground almonds
30ml/2 tbsp chopped
   fresh coriander (cilantro)
good pinch of paprika
pinch of cayenne pepper

1 Preheat the oven to 180°C/350°F/Gas 4. To make the stuffing, place the couscous in a bowl and pour the chicken stock over it. Stir with a fork and set aside for 10 minutes to swell.

2 Meanwhile, melt the butter in a small frying pan and fry the shallot for 2–3 minutes until soft. Fluff up the couscous, and stir in the shallot and all the butter from the pan. Add the remaining stuffing ingredients, season and stir well.

3 Loosely push the couscous mixture into the neck end of the chicken and truss the bird neatly.

4 Blend the ginger and cinnamon with the saffron water. Rub the chicken with salt and pepper, and then pour over the saffron water. Place the chicken in a small roasting pan or dish so that it fits snugly. Spoon the chopped onions and stock around the edge, and then cover the dish with foil, pinching the foil around the edges of the dish firmly so that the chicken sits in a foil "tent".

5 Cook in the oven for 1¼ hours, then increase the oven temperature to 200°C/400°F/Gas 6. Transfer the chicken to a plate and strain the cooking liquid into a jug (pitcher), reserving the chopped onions. Place the chicken back in the roasting pan with the onions, baste with a little of the cooking liquid and sprinkle with the flaked almonds.

6 Return to the oven and cook for about 30 minutes until the chicken is golden brown and the juices run clear when the thickest part of the thigh is pierced with a knife or skewer.

7 Pour off the fat from the reserved cooking juices and pour into a small pan. Blend the flour with 30ml/2 tbsp water, stir into the pan with the cooking juices and heat gently, stirring to make a smooth sauce. Garnish the chicken with lemon wedges and coriander and serve with the sauce.

Harissa-spiced Roast Chicken

The spices and fruit in the stuffing give this chicken an unusual flavour.

Serves 4–5
1.5kg/3½lb chicken
30–60ml/2–4 tbsp garlic and
    spice aromatic oil
a few bay leaves
10ml/2 tsp clear honey
10ml/2 tsp tomato purée (paste)
60ml/4 tbsp lemon juice
150ml/¼ pint/⅔ cup
    chicken stock
2.5–5ml/½–1 tsp harissa

For the stuffing
25g/1oz/2 tbsp butter
1 onion, chopped
1 garlic clove, crushed
7.5ml/1½ tsp ground cinnamon
2.5ml/½ tsp ground cumin
225g/8oz/1⅓ cups dried fruit,
    soaked for several hours or
    overnight in water to cover
25g/1oz/¼ cup blanched
    almonds, finely chopped
salt and freshly ground
    black pepper

1 To make the stuffing, melt the butter in a pan. Add the onion and garlic, and cook gently for 5 minutes until soft. Add the cinnamon and cumin and cook, stirring, for 2 minutes. Drain the dried fruit, chop it roughly and add to the stuffing with the almonds. Season with salt and pepper, and cook for 2 minutes more. Tip into a bowl and leave to cool.

2 Preheat the oven to 200°C/400°F/Gas 6. Stuff the neck of the chicken with the fruit mixture, reserving any excess. Brush the garlic and spice oil over the chicken. Place the chicken in a roasting pan, tuck in the bay leaves and roast for about 1–1¼ hours, basting occasionally, until the juices run clear when the thickest part of the thigh is pierced with a knife or skewer.

3 Transfer the chicken to a carving board. Pour off any excess fat from the roasting pan. Stir the honey, tomato purée, lemon juice, stock and harissa into the juices in the roasting pan. Add salt to taste. Bring to the boil, lower the heat and simmer for 2 minutes, stirring frequently.

4 Reheat any excess stuffing. Carve the chicken, pour the sauce into a small bowl and serve with the stuffing and chicken.

Sunday Roast Chicken

As you might expect, rum features in the glaze for this Caribbean-style roast.

Serves 6
1.5kg/3½lb chicken
5ml/1 tsp paprika
5ml/1 tsp dried thyme
2.5ml/½ tsp dried tarragon
5ml/1 tsp garlic granules
15ml/1 tbsp lemon juice
30ml/2 tbsp clear honey
45ml/3 tbsp dark rum
melted butter, for basting
300ml/½ pint/1¼ cups
    chicken stock
salt and freshly ground
    black pepper
lime quarters and fresh herbs,
    to garnish

1 Place the chicken in a roasting pan and sprinkle with the paprika, thyme, tarragon, garlic granules and salt and pepper. Rub the mixture all over the chicken, lifting the skin and spreading the seasoning underneath it too. Cover loosely with clear film (plastic wrap) and leave to marinate in a cool place for at least 2 hours or preferably overnight in the refrigerator.

2 Preheat the oven to 190°C/375°F/Gas 5. Blend together the lemon juice, honey and rum and pour over and under the skin of the chicken, rubbing it in well.

3 Spoon the melted butter over the chicken, then roast for 1½–2 hours or until the juices run clear when the thickest part of the thigh is pierced with a skewer or knife.

4 Transfer the chicken to a warmed serving platter and leave to rest while you make the gravy. Pour the juices from the roasting pan into a small pan. Add the stock and simmer over a low heat for 10 minutes or until reduced. Adjust the seasoning and pour into a jug (pitcher). Serve with the chicken, garnished with lime quarters and herbs.

Cook's Tip
Extra herbs and rum can be used to make a richer, tastier gravy, if you like.

Spicy Roast Chicken

Roasting chicken like this in an oven that has not been preheated produces a particularly crispy skin.

Serves 4
1.5kg/3½lb chicken
juice of 1 lemon
4 garlic cloves, finely chopped

15ml/1 tbsp each cayenne
    pepper, paprika and
    dried oregano
10ml/2 tsp olive oil
salt and freshly ground
    black pepper
fresh coriander (cilantro) sprigs,
    to garnish
sliced (bell) peppers, to serve

1 Using a sharp knife or poultry shears, remove the backbone from the chicken. Turn it breast-side up. With the heel of your hand, press down firmly to break the breastbone and open the chicken out flat like an open book. Insert a metal skewer through the width of the chicken, at the thighs, to keep it flat during cooking.

2 Place the chicken in a shallow dish and pour over the lemon juice. Place the garlic, cayenne, paprika, oregano, black pepper and oil in a small bowl and mix well. Rub evenly over the surface of the chicken.

3 Cover the chicken and leave to marinate for 2–3 hours at room temperature, or chill the chicken overnight and then return to room temperature before roasting.

4 Season both sides of the chicken with salt and place it, skin-side up, in a shallow roasting pan.

5 Set the oven temperature to 200°C/400°F/Gas 6. Roast the chicken for about 1 hour until it is done, basting with the juices in the pan. To test whether the chicken is cooked, prick the thickest part of the flesh with a skewer or knife: the juices that run out should be clear. Serve the chicken hot, garnished with coriander sprigs and accompanied by mixed peppers.

East African Roast Chicken

Smothered in a generous layer of butter combined with spices, herbs and coconut milk, this chicken is left to stand overnight to allow the flavours to mingle.

Serves 6
1.75kg/4lb chicken
30ml/2 tbsp softened butter, plus
    extra for basting
3 garlic cloves, crushed

5ml/1 tsp freshly ground
    black pepper
5ml/1 tsp ground turmeric
2.5ml/½ tsp ground cumin
5ml/1 tsp dried thyme
15ml/1 tbsp finely chopped fresh
    coriander (cilantro)
60ml/4 tbsp thick coconut milk
60ml/4 tbsp medium-dry sherry
5ml/1 tsp tomato purée (paste)
salt and chilli powder
fresh coriander (cilantro) leaves,
    to garnish

1 Remove the giblets from the chicken, if necessary, rinse out the cavity and pat the skin dry.

2 Put the butter and all the remaining ingredients in a bowl and mix together well to form a thick paste.

3 Gently ease the skin of the chicken away from the flesh and rub the flesh generously with the herb and butter mixture. Rub more of the mixture over the skin, legs and wings of the chicken and into the neck cavity. Place the chicken in a roasting pan, cover loosely with foil and leave to marinate overnight in the refrigerator.

4 Preheat the oven to 190°C/375°F/Gas 5. Cover the chicken with clean foil and roast for 1 hour, then turn the chicken over and baste with the roasting juices. Cover again with foil and cook for 30 minutes.

5 Remove the foil and place the chicken breast side up. Rub with a little extra butter and roast for a further 10–15 minutes until the juices run clear when the thickest part of the thigh is pierced with a skewer or knife and the skin is golden brown. Allow the chicken to rest for 10–15 minutes in a warm place before serving, garnished with coriander leaves.

Chicken with Lentils & Coconut

This delicious, tangy chicken stew comes from Kenya. The amount of lemon juice can be reduced, if you prefer a less sharp sauce.

Serves 4–6
6 chicken thighs or portions
2.5–3.5ml/ ½–¾ tsp ground ginger
50g/2oz/ ¼ cup mung beans
60ml/4 tbsp corn oil
2 onions, finely chopped
2 garlic cloves, crushed
5 tomatoes, peeled and chopped
1 fresh green chilli, seeded and finely chopped
30ml/2 tbsp lemon juice
300ml/ ½ pint/1¼ cups coconut milk
300ml/ ½ pint/1¼ cups water
15ml/1 tbsp chopped fresh coriander (cilantro)
salt and freshly ground black pepper
cooked green vegetable and rice or chapatis, to serve

1 Season the chicken pieces with the ginger and a little salt and freshly ground pepper, and set aside in a cool place to allow the spices to penetrate the meat. Meanwhile, boil the mung beans in plenty of water for 35 minutes until soft, then mash well.

2 Heat the oil in a large pan over a moderate heat and fry the chicken pieces, in batches if necessary, until evenly browned. Transfer to a plate and set aside, reserving the oil and chicken juices in the pan.

3 In the same pan, fry the onions and garlic for 5 minutes, then add the tomatoes and chilli, and cook for a further 1–2 minutes, stirring well.

4 Add the mashed mung beans, lemon juice and coconut milk to the pan. Simmer for 5 minutes, then add the chicken pieces and a little water if the sauce is too thick. Stir in the chopped coriander and simmer for about 35 minutes until the chicken is cooked through.

5 Taste and adjust the seasoning as necessary. Serve with a green vegetable and rice or chapatis.

Chicken with Pimientos

In this Mediterranean Jewish recipe, chicken is cooked in the oven with sweet red (bell) peppers, or pimientos.

Serves 6
2kg/4½lb chicken
3 ripe tomatoes
2 large red (bell) peppers or pimientos
15ml/1 tbsp Spanish paprika
60–90ml/4–6 tbsp olive oil
1 large onion, sliced
2 garlic cloves, crushed
15ml/1 tbsp sugar
salt and freshly ground black pepper
fresh flat leaf parsley, to garnish
boiled rice and black olives, to serve

1 Preheat the oven to 190°C/375°F/Gas 5. Joint the chicken and cut into 6 pieces; set aside. Peel and chop the tomatoes, and seed and slice the red peppers.

2 Heat half of the oil in a large, heavy frying pan and sauté the onion, garlic, paprika and red peppers for 3 minutes. Transfer to an ovenproof dish.

3 Add the chicken pieces to the frying pan, with a little more oil if necessary, and fry until browned all over. Add to the vegetables in the dish.

4 Fry the tomatoes in the remaining oil for a few minutes. Add the sugar, seasoning and 15ml/1 tbsp water, then spoon the mixture over the chicken.

5 Cook, uncovered, in the oven for about 1 hour. Cover if the chicken is getting too brown. Halfway through, pour the juices into a jug (pitcher) and leave to stand.

6 Serve the chicken with boiled rice and black olives, garnished with flat leaf parsley. Skim the fat off the juices, reheat and hand round as extra gravy.

Thyme & Lime Chicken

Chicken thighs, stuffed with spring onion, are coated in butter flavoured with lime, chilli and herbs.

Serves 4

8 chicken thighs
30ml/2 tbsp chopped spring
    onion (scallion)
5ml/1 tsp dried or chopped
    fresh thyme
2 garlic cloves, crushed
15ml/1 tbsp chilli powder
juice of 1 lime
90ml/6 tbsp melted butter
salt and freshly ground
    black pepper
lime slices, chopped spring onions
    (scallions) and fresh coriander
    (cilantro) sprigs, to garnish
cooked rice, to serve

1 Put the chicken thighs in an ovenproof dish skin-side down and, using a sharp knife, make a slit lengthways along each thigh bone. Mix the spring onion with a little salt and pepper, and press the mixture into the slits.

2 Mix together the thyme, garlic, chilli, lime juice and all but 30ml/2 tbsp of the melted butter in a small bowl and spoon a little over each chicken thigh.

3 Spoon the remaining butter over the top. Cover the chicken loosely with clear film (plastic wrap) and set aside to marinate in a cool place for several hours or overnight in the refrigerator.

4 Preheat the oven to 190°C/375°F/Gas 5. Remove the clear film from the chicken and cover the dish with foil. Bake for 1 hour, then remove the foil and cook for a few more minutes to brown. Serve hot, garnished with lime, spring onions and coriander, and accompanied by rice.

> **Cook's Tip**
> *You may need to use two limes, depending on their size and juiciness. Or, for a less sharp flavour, use lemons instead.*

Palava Chicken

A variation of a popular Ghanaian dish, which was originally made from fish. In Sierra Leone, peanut butter is often added.

Serves 4

675g/1½ lb skinless chicken
    breast fillets
2 garlic cloves, crushed
30ml/2 tbsp butter or margarine
30ml/2 tbsp palm or vegetable oil
1 onion, finely chopped
4 tomatoes, peeled and chopped
30ml/2 tbsp peanut butter
600ml/1 pint/2½ cups chicken
    stock or water
1 fresh thyme sprig or 5ml/1 tsp
    dried thyme
225g/8oz frozen leaf spinach,
    thawed and chopped
1 fresh chilli, seeded and chopped
salt and freshly ground
    black pepper
boiled yams, to serve

1 Cut the chicken fillets into thin slices, place in a bowl and stir in the garlic and a little salt and pepper. Melt the butter or margarine in a large frying pan and fry the chicken over a moderate heat, turning once or twice to brown evenly. Transfer to a plate, using a slotted spoon, and set aside.

2 Heat the oil in a large pan, and fry the onion and tomatoes over a high heat for 5 minutes until soft. Reduce the heat, add the peanut butter and half of the stock or water and blend together well.

3 Cook for 4–5 minutes, stirring constantly to prevent the peanut butter from burning, then add the remaining stock or water, the thyme, spinach, chilli and seasoning. Stir in the chicken slices and cook over a moderate heat for about 10–15 minutes until the chicken is cooked through. Pour into a warmed serving dish and serve with boiled yams.

> **Cook's Tip**
> *If you have time, fresh spinach adds a fresher flavour. Egusi – ground melon seed – can be used instead of peanut butter.*

Chicken with Chorizo

The addition of chorizo sausage and sherry gives a warm, interesting flavour to this simple Spanish casserole. Serve with rice or boiled potatoes.

Serves 4

1 medium chicken, jointed, or
  4 chicken legs, halved
10ml/2 tsp ground paprika
60ml/4 tbsp olive oil
2 small onions, sliced
6 garlic cloves, thinly sliced
150g/5oz chorizo sausage, sliced
400g/14oz can
  chopped tomatoes
12–16 bay leaves
75ml/5 tbsp medium sherry
salt and freshly ground
  black pepper
boiled rice or potatoes, to serve

1 Preheat the oven to 190°C/375°F/Gas 5. Coat the chicken pieces in the paprika, making sure that they are evenly covered, then season with salt. Heat the olive oil in a frying pan and fry the chicken until brown.

2 Transfer to an ovenproof dish. Add the onions to the pan and fry over a medium heat for 5 minutes. Add the garlic and sliced chorizo, and fry for about 2 minutes.

3 Add the tomatoes, 2 of the bay leaves and the sherry, and bring to the boil. Pour over the chicken and cover with a lid. Bake for 45 minutes.

4 Remove the lid and season to taste. Cook for a further 20 minutes until the chicken is tender and golden. Serve with rice or potatoes, garnished with bay leaves.

Variation

For a Portuguese version of this dish, substitute linguica for the chorizo and white port for the sherry.

Chicken Rendang

This marvellous Malaysian dish is great served with deep-fried anchovies.

Serves 4

4 skinless chicken breast fillets
5ml/1 tsp sugar
75g/3oz/1 cup desiccated
  (dry, unsweetened
  shredded) coconut
4 small red or white onions,
  roughly chopped
2 garlic cloves, chopped
2.5cm/1in piece fresh root
  ginger, sliced
1–2 lemon grass stalks,
  root trimmed
2.5cm/1in piece galangal, peeled
  and sliced
75ml/5 tbsp groundnut (peanut)
  oil or vegetable oil
10–15ml/2–3 tsp chilli powder,
  or to taste
400ml/14fl oz can coconut milk
about 10ml/2 tsp salt
fresh chives and deep-fried
  anchovies, to garnish

1 Halve the chicken breast fillets, sprinkle with the sugar and leave to stand for about 1 hour.

2 Dry-fry the coconut in a wok over a low heat, turning constantly, until crisp and golden. Transfer to a food processor and process to an oily paste. Transfer to a bowl and reserve.

3 Add the onions, garlic and ginger to the processor. Cut off the lower 5cm/2in of the lemon grass, chop and add to the processor with the galangal. Process to a fine paste.

4 Heat the oil in a wok or large pan. Fry the onion mixture for a few minutes. Reduce the heat, stir in the chilli powder and cook for 2–3 minutes, stirring. Spoon in 120ml/4fl oz/ ½ cup of the coconut milk, with salt to taste. As soon as the mixture bubbles, add the chicken, turning until well coated with the spices. Pour in the remaining coconut milk, stirring. Bruise the top of the lemon grass stalks and add to the wok or pan. Cover and cook over a low heat for 40–45 minutes until the chicken is tender.

5 Stir in the reserved coconut paste. Bring to just below boiling point, then simmer for 5 minutes. Transfer to a serving bowl, and garnish with chives and deep-fried anchovies. Serve immediately.

Chicken Thighs Wrapped in Bacon

These tasty chicken "parcels" are first marinated and then baked in a spicy garlic and citrus sauce.

Serves 4
16 bacon rashers (strips), rinded
8 skinless chicken thighs
cooked rice, to serve

For the marinade
finely grated rind and juice of
* 1 orange*
finely grated rind and juice of
* 1 lime*
5 garlic cloves, finely chopped
15ml/1 tbsp chilli powder
15ml/1 tbsp paprika
5ml/1 tsp ground cumin
2.5ml/ ½ tsp dried oregano
15ml/1 tbsp olive oil

1 To make the marinade, combine the citrus rind and juice, garlic, chilli powder, paprika, cumin, oregano and olive oil in a small bowl.

2 Wrap 2 rashers of bacon around each chicken thigh in a cross shape. Secure with wooden cocktail sticks or toothpicks. Arrange the chicken thighs in an ovenproof dish.

3 Pour the marinade over the chicken, cover with clear film (plastic wrap) and set aside for 1 hour at room temperature or for several hours in the refrigerator.

4 Preheat the oven to 190°C/375°F/Gas 5. Place the dish in the oven and bake until the chicken is cooked through and the bacon is crisp: this will take about 40 minutes for small thighs and 1 hour for large thighs. Skim excess fat from the sauce and serve with rice.

> **Cook's Tip**
> *Chilli powder varies widely in strength, although it is always hot, and some varieties have other spices or herbs added. It is best to buy pure ground chilli powder and add your own flavourings if you want to.*

Aromatic Chicken from Madura

An Indonesian dish which is best cooked ahead so that the flavours permeate the chicken flesh, making it even more delicious.

Serves 4
1.5kg/3½lb chicken, cut into
  quarters, or 4 chicken quarters
5ml/1 tsp sugar
30ml/2 tbsp coriander seeds
10ml/2 tsp cumin seeds
6 whole cloves
2.5ml/ ½ tsp grated nutmeg
2.5ml/ ½ tsp ground turmeric
1 small onion
2.5cm/1in piece fresh root
  ginger, sliced
300ml/ ½ pint/1¼ cups chicken
  stock or water
salt and freshly ground
  black pepper
boiled rice and deep-fried
  onions, to serve

1 Cut each chicken quarter in half. Place in a flameproof casserole, sprinkle with sugar and salt and toss together.

2 Dry-fry the coriander, cumin and whole cloves in a heavy frying pan until the spices give off a good aroma. Add the nutmeg and turmeric, and heat briefly. Grind in a food processor or using a pestle and mortar.

3 If using a processor, process the onion and ginger until finely chopped. Otherwise, finely chop the onion and ginger and pound to a paste using a pestle and mortar. Add the spices and stock or water and mix well. Season to taste.

4 Pour the mixture over the chicken in the casserole. Cover and cook over a low heat for about 45–50 minutes until the chicken pieces are really tender. Serve portions of the chicken, with the sauce, on a bed of boiled rice, scattered with crisp deep-fried onions.

> **Cook's Tip**
> *Add a large piece of bruised ginger and a small onion to the chicken stock to ensure a good flavour.*

Chicken Provençal

A richly flavoured dish in which the chicken and vegetables are simmered slowly together until wonderfully tender.

Serves 4

1 medium aubergine
   (eggplant), diced
10ml/2 tsp olive oil
8 skinless chicken thighs
1 medium red onion, cut
   into wedges
1 green (bell) pepper, seeded and
   thickly sliced
2 garlic cloves, sliced
1 small fresh green chilli, sliced
2 courgettes (zucchini),
   thickly sliced
2 beefsteak tomatoes, cut
   into wedges
1 bouquet garni
salt and freshly ground
   black pepper

1 Sprinkle the aubergine with salt, then leave to drain for 30 minutes. Rinse and pat dry with kitchen paper.

2 Heat the oil in a large, non-stick pan and fry the chicken until golden. Add the aubergine, onion, green pepper and garlic, and fry gently until the vegetables are soft.

3 Add the chilli, courgettes, tomatoes, bouquet garni and seasoning. Cover tightly and cook over a low heat for 25–30 minutes until the chicken and vegetables are tender. Remove the bouquet garni and serve immediately.

> **Cook's Tip**
> In the past, it was always necessary to sprinkle aubergines with salt to remove the bitter and unpalatable juices. Modern varieties, especially those grown under glass, have been selectively bred so that this is rarely essential. Nevertheless, it is worth doing if the aubergine is to be fried as it helps to reduce the amount of oil absorbed and improves the texture. Always rinse the aubergines to get rid of all traces of salt and then pat dry before using.

Caribbean Ginger Chicken

Pineapple helps to keep the chicken moist during cooking, as well as providing flavour along with the other ingredients, without the addition of any fat. Pineapple also contains an enzyme that helps to tenderize meat.

Serves 4

4 skinless chicken breast portions
1/2 small fresh pineapple, peeled
   and sliced
2 spring onions
   (scallions), chopped
30ml/2 tbsp chopped fresh
   root ginger
1 garlic clove, crushed
15ml/1 tbsp dark
   muscovado (molasses) sugar
15ml/1 tbsp lime juice
5ml/1 tsp hot pepper sauce
5ml/1 tsp tomato purée (paste)
salt and freshly ground
   black pepper
cooked plain and wild rice, and
   salad, to serve

1 Preheat the oven to 200°C/400°F/Gas 6. Slash the chicken at intervals with a sharp knife. Place in an ovenproof dish with the pineapple slices.

2 Mix together the chopped spring onions, ginger, crushed garlic, sugar, lime juice, pepper sauce, tomato purée in a bowl and season with salt and pepper to taste. Spread the mixture over the chicken.

3 Cover and bake for 30 minutes or until the chicken juices run clear when the thickest part is pierced with a skewer or knife. Serve with plain and wild rice, and salad.

> **Cook's Tip**
> To prepare fresh pineapple, cut off the green spiky top and take a thin slice from the base, so that it will stand upright. Using a sharp, long-bladed knife, cut off the skin downwards in wide strips. Carefully remove the hard brown "eyes" from the pineapple flesh with the point of the knife. Cut the flesh into slices, then remove the woody core from each slice with a knife.

Peanut Chicken

In this Caribbean dish the rich, nutty sauce is best made from smooth peanut butter, but it can also be made with crushed peanuts.

Serves 4

900g/2lb skinless chicken breast
   fillets, cut into pieces
2 garlic cloves, crushed
2.5ml/ ½ tsp dried thyme
2.5ml/ ½ tsp freshly ground
   black pepper
15ml/1 tbsp curry powder
15ml/1 tbsp lemon juice
25g/1oz/2 tbsp butter
   or margarine
1 onion, chopped
45ml/3 tbsp chopped tomatoes
1 fresh hot chilli, chopped
30ml/2 tbsp smooth
   peanut butter
about 450ml/ ¾ pint/scant 2 cups
   warm water
salt
fresh coriander (cilantro) sprigs,
   to garnish
fried plantain, to serve

1 Place the chicken pieces in a large bowl and stir in the garlic, thyme, pepper, curry powder, lemon juice and a little salt. Cover loosely with clear film (plastic wrap) and set aside to marinate in a cool place for a few hours.

2 Melt the butter or margarine in a large pan, add the onion and sauté gently for 5 minutes. Add the seasoned chicken and fry over a medium heat for 10 minutes, turning frequently. Stir in the tomatoes and chilli.

3 Blend the peanut butter with a little of the warm water to a smooth paste and stir into the chicken mixture.

4 Gradually stir in the remaining water, then simmer gently for about 30 minutes, adding a little more water if necessary. Garnish with coriander sprigs and serve immediately with fried plantain.

> **Variation**
> You could substitute lime juice for the lemon juice and add 5ml/1 tsp ground allspice with the curry powder.

Chicken Sauce Piquante

Cajun Sauce Piquante is based on the brown Cajun *roux* and has chilli peppers to give it heat.

Serves 4

4 chicken legs or 2 legs and
   2 breast portions
75ml/5 tbsp cooking oil
50g/2oz/ ½ cup plain (all-
   purpose) flour
1 medium onion, chopped
1 green (bell) pepper, seeded
   and diced
2 celery sticks, sliced
2 garlic cloves, crushed
1 bay leaf
2.5ml/ ½ tsp dried thyme
2.5ml/ ½ tsp dried oregano
1–2 fresh red chilli peppers,
   seeded and finely chopped
400g/14oz can chopped
   tomatoes, with their juice
300ml/ ½ pint/1 ¼ cups
   chicken stock
salt and freshly ground
   black pepper
watercress or fresh parsley,
   to garnish
boiled potatoes, to serve

1 Halve the chicken legs through the joint, or the breast portions across the middle, to give 8 pieces. In a heavy frying pan, fry the chicken pieces in the oil until brown on all sides, lifting them out and setting them aside as they are done.

2 Strain the oil from the pan into a flameproof casserole. Heat it and stir in the flour. Stir constantly over a low heat until the *roux* is the colour of peanut butter. Immediately the *roux* reaches this stage, tip in the onion, green pepper and celery and stir over the heat for 2–3 minutes.

3 Add the garlic, bay leaf, thyme, oregano and chilli pepper(s). Stir for 1 minute, then lower the heat and stir in the tomatoes with their juice.

4 Gradually stir in the stock. Add the chicken pieces, cover and simmer for 45 minutes until the chicken is tender.

5 If there is too much sauce or it is too runny, remove the lid for the last 10–15 minutes of the cooking time and raise the heat a little. Adjust the seasoning to taste and serve, garnished with watercress or parsley and accompanied by boiled potatoes.

Adobo of Chicken & Pork

Four ingredients are essential in an adobo, one of the best-loved recipes in the Filipino repertoire: vinegar, garlic, peppercorns and bay leaves.

Serves 4

1.3kg/3lb chicken or
   4 chicken quarters
350g/12oz pork leg steaks
10ml/2 tsp sugar
60ml/4 tbsp sunflower oil
75ml/5 tbsp wine vinegar or
   cider vinegar
4 plump garlic cloves, crushed
2.5ml/ 1/2 tsp black peppercorns,
   lightly crushed
15ml/1 tbsp light soy sauce
4 bay leaves
2.5ml/ 1/2 tsp annatto seeds,
   soaked in 30ml/2 tbsp boiling
   water, or 2.5ml/ 1/2 tsp
   ground turmeric
salt

For the plantain chips (fries)

vegetable oil, for deep-frying
1–2 large plantains and/or
   1 sweet potato

1 Wipe the chicken and cut into 8 pieces or halve the chicken quarters, if using. Cut the pork into neat pieces. Spread the meat out on a board, sprinkle lightly with sugar and set aside.

2 Heat the oil in a wok or large frying pan, and fry the chicken and pork pieces, in batches if necessary, until golden all over.

3 Add the vinegar, garlic, peppercorns, soy sauce and bay leaves and stir well. Strain the annatto seed liquid and stir it into the pan or stir in the turmeric. Add salt to taste. Bring to the boil, cover, lower the heat and simmer for 30–35 minutes. Remove the lid and simmer for a further 10 minutes.

4 Meanwhile, to make the plantain chips, heat the oil in a deep-fryer to 195°C/383°F. Peel the plantains and/or sweet potato and slice into rounds. Deep-fry them, in batches if necessary, until cooked but not brown. Drain on kitchen paper.

5 When ready to serve, reheat the oil and fry the plantains or sweet potato until crisp. Drain. Spoon the adobo into a serving dish and serve with the chips.

Chicken & Olives

A whole chicken is simmered gently with fresh root ginger, paprika and saffron, and finished with lemon juice and green and black olives.

Serves 4

30ml/2 tbsp olive oil
1.5kg/3 1/2 lb chicken
1 large onion, sliced
15ml/1 tbsp grated fresh
   root ginger
3 garlic cloves, crushed
5ml/1 tsp paprika
250ml/8fl oz/1 cup chicken stock
2–3 saffron threads, soaked in
   15ml/1 tbsp boiling water
4–5 spring onions
   (scallions), chopped
15–20 black and green olives,
   stoned (pitted)
juice of 1/2 lemon
salt and freshly ground
   black pepper
boiled rice and mixed salad,
   to serve

1 Heat the oil in a large pan or flameproof casserole. Add the chicken and sauté until golden on all sides.

2 Add the onion, ginger, garlic and paprika, and season to taste with salt and pepper. Continue to fry over a moderate heat, coating the chicken with the mixture.

3 Add the chicken stock and saffron, and bring to the boil. Cover, lower the heat and simmer gently for 45 minutes.

4 Add the chopped spring onions and cook for a further 15 minutes until the chicken is well cooked and the sauce is reduced to about 120ml/4fl oz/ 1/2 cup. The chicken juices should run clear when the thickest part of the thigh is pierced. Add the olives and lemon juice and cook for a further 5 minutes.

5 Transfer the chicken to a large, deep serving plate and pour over the sauce. Serve immediately with rice and a mixed salad.

Chicken with Turmeric

Colourful, aromatic and creamy, this is a perfect dish to serve to guests for an informal supper.

Serves 4

1.5kg/3½lb chicken, cut into
    8 pieces, or 4 chicken quarters,
    each halved
15ml/1 tbsp sugar
3 macadamia nuts or 6 almonds
2 garlic cloves, crushed
1 large onion, quartered
2.5cm/1in piece fresh galangal,
    peeled and sliced, or 5ml/1 tsp
    powdered galangal

1–2 lemon grass stalks, lower
    5cm/2in sliced, top bruised
1cm/½in cube terasi (fermented
    shrimp paste)
4cm/1½in piece fresh turmeric,
    peeled and sliced, or 15ml/
    1 tbsp ground turmeric
15ml/1 tbsp tamarind pulp,
    soaked in 150ml/¼ pint/⅔ cup
    warm water
60–90ml/4–6 tbsp oil
400ml/14fl oz/1⅔ cups
    coconut milk
salt and freshly ground
    black pepper
deep-fried onions, to garnish

1 Rub the chicken joints with a little sugar and set them aside.

2 Grind the nuts and garlic in a food processor with the onion, galangal, sliced lemon grass, *terasi* and turmeric. Alternatively, pound the ingredients to a paste using a pestle and mortar. Strain the tamarind pulp and reserve the juice. Discard the contents of the strainer.

3 Heat the oil in a wok or heavy frying pan and cook the paste, without browning, until it gives off a spicy aroma. Add the pieces of chicken and toss well in the spices. Add the strained tamarind juice.

4 Spoon the coconut cream off the top of the milk and set it to one side. Add the coconut milk to the pan. Cover and cook for 45 minutes or until the chicken is tender.

5 Just before serving, stir in the reserved coconut cream while bringing to the boil. Season to taste with salt and pepper, and serve at once, garnished with deep-fried onions.

Mole Poblano de Guajolote

This is the greatest festive dish of Mexico, served at any special occasion. The traditional accompaniments are rice, beans, tortillas and guacamole.

Serves 6–8

2.75–3.6kg/6–8lb turkey, cut into
    serving portions
1 onion, chopped
1 garlic clove, chopped
90ml/6 tbsp lard (shortening) or
    corn oil
salt
fresh coriander (cilantro) and
    30ml/2 tbsp toasted sesame
    seeds, to garnish

For the sauce
6 dried ancho chillies
4 dried pasilla chillies
4 dried mulato chillies

1 drained canned chipotle chilli,
    seeded and chopped (optional)
2 onions, chopped
2 garlic cloves, chopped
450g/1lb tomatoes, peeled
    and chopped
1 stale tortilla, torn into pieces
50g/2oz/⅓ cup seedless raisins
115g/4oz/1 cup ground almonds
45ml/3 tbsp sesame
    seeds, ground
5ml/1 tsp ground cinnamon
2.5ml/½ tsp ground anise
1.5ml/¼ tsp ground
    black peppercorns
60ml/4 tbsp lard (shortening) or
    corn oil
40g/1½oz unsweetened
    chocolate, broken into squares
15ml/1 tbsp sugar
salt and freshly ground
    black pepper

1 Put the turkey into a large flameproof casserole in one layer. Add the onion, garlic and enough cold water to cover. Season with salt, bring to a gentle simmer, cover and cook for 1 hour.

2 Lift the turkey out of the casserole and pat dry with kitchen paper. Reserve the stock. Heat the lard or oil in a frying pan and sauté the turkey until lightly browned all over. Transfer to a plate and set aside. Reserve the oil in the pan.

3 Meanwhile, to make the sauce, put the dried chillies in a dry frying pan over a gentle heat and roast them for a few minutes, shaking the pan frequently. Remove the stems and shake out the seeds. Tear the pods into pieces and put these into a small bowl. Add sufficient warm water just to cover and soak, turning from time to time, for 30 minutes until soft.

4 Tip the chillies with their soaking water into a food processor. Add the *chipotle* chilli, if using, with the onions, garlic, tomatoes, tortilla, raisins, ground almonds, ground sesame seeds and spices. Process to a purée. Do this in batches if necessary.

5 Add the lard or oil to the fat remaining in the frying pan used for sautéing the turkey. Heat the mixture, then add the chilli and spice paste. Cook, stirring, for 5 minutes.

6 Transfer the spice mixture to the casserole in which the turkey was originally cooked. Stir in 475ml/16fl oz/2 cups of the reserved stock (make it up with water if necessary). Add the chocolate and season with salt and pepper. Cook over a low heat until the chocolate has melted. Stir in the sugar. Add the turkey to the casserole and more stock if needed. Cover and simmer gently for 30 minutes. Serve, garnished with fresh coriander and sprinkled with toasted sesame seeds.

Chicken Bobotie

Perfect for a buffet party, this mild curry dish is set with savoury custard, which makes serving easy.

Serves 8

2 thick slices white bread
450ml/¾ pint/scant 2 cups milk
30ml/2 tbsp olive oil
2 medium onions, finely chopped
40ml/2½ tbsp medium
 curry powder
1.2kg/2½ lb minced
 (ground) chicken
15ml/1 tbsp apricot jam, chutney
 or caster (superfine) sugar
30ml/2 tbsp wine vinegar or
 lemon juice
3 large (US extra large)
 eggs, beaten
50g/2oz/⅓ cup raisins or
 sultanas (golden raisins)
butter, for greasing
12 almonds
salt and freshly ground
 black pepper
boiled rice, to serve

1 Preheat the oven to 180°C/350°F/Gas 4. Soak the bread in 150ml/¼ pint/⅔ cup of the milk.

2 Heat the oil in a frying pan and fry the onions until tender. Add the curry powder and cook for a further 2 minutes. Add the minced chicken and brown all over, stirring to break up any lumps. Remove from the heat, season and add the apricot jam, chutney or sugar and vinegar or lemon juice.

3 Mash the bread in the milk and add to the pan with one of the beaten eggs and the raisins or sultanas.

4 Grease a 1.5 litre/2½ pint/6¼ cup shallow ovenproof dish with butter. Spoon in the chicken mixture and level the top. Cover with buttered foil and bake for 30 minutes.

5 Meanwhile, beat the remaining eggs with the rest of the milk. Remove the dish from the oven and lower the temperature to 150°C/300°F/Gas 2. Break up the meat using two forks and pour over the beaten egg mixture. Scatter the almonds over the top and return to the oven to bake, uncovered, for 30 minutes until set and golden brown all over. Serve immediately with rice.

Tagine of Chicken

Based on a traditional Moroccan recipe, this spicy chicken stew is served with vegetable couscous.

Serves 8

30ml/2 tbsp olive oil
8 chicken legs, cut in half
1 medium onion, finely chopped
2 garlic cloves, crushed
5ml/1 tsp ground turmeric
2.5ml/½ tsp ground ginger
2.5ml/½ tsp ground cinnamon
450ml/¾ pint/scant 2 cups
 chicken stock
150g/5oz/1¼ cups pitted
 green olives
1 lemon, sliced
salt and freshly ground
 black pepper
fresh coriander (cilantro) sprigs,
 to garnish

For the vegetable couscous

600ml/1 pint/2½ cups
 chicken stock
450g/1lb/2⅔ cups couscous
4 courgettes (zucchini),
 thickly sliced
2 carrots, thickly sliced
2 small turnips, cubed
45ml/3 tbsp olive oil
425g/15oz can chickpeas, rinsed
15ml/1 tbsp chopped
 fresh coriander (cilantro)

1 Preheat the oven to 180°C/350°F/Gas 4. Heat the oil in a flameproof casserole and brown the chicken all over. Remove from the casserole and keep warm. Add the onion and garlic to the casserole and cook until tender. Add the spices and cook for 1 minute. Pour in the stock and bring to the boil. Return the chicken to the casserole. Cover and bake for 45 minutes.

2 Transfer the chicken to a bowl, cover and keep warm. Skim any fat from the cooking liquid and boil to reduce by one-third.

3 Meanwhile, blanch the olives and lemon slices in boiling water for 2 minutes. Drain and add to the casserole. Season to taste.

4 To make the vegetable couscous, bring the stock to the boil in a large pan and sprinkle in the couscous slowly, stirring. Remove from the heat, cover and set aside for 5 minutes. Cook the vegetables, drain and place in a bowl. Add the couscous, oil and seasoning. Stir the grains and add the remaining ingredients. Garnish and serve the couscous with the chicken and sauce.

Stuffed Turkey in Lemon Sauce

Sweet potatoes and prawns (shrimp) flavoured with herbs and chilli make an unusual and tasty stuffing for turkey fillets.

Serves 4

175g/6oz sweet potato
1 onion, finely chopped
5ml/1 tsp dried tarragon, crushed
2.5ml/½ tsp dried basil
1 fresh green chilli, seeded and finely chopped
1 garlic clove, crushed
2.5ml/½ tsp dried thyme
115g/4oz peeled cooked prawns (shrimp), chopped
4 turkey fillets, about 225g/8oz each

butter, for greasing
salt and freshly ground black pepper
cooked root vegetables, bulgur wheat or rice, to serve

For the lemon sauce

15ml/1 tbsp olive oil
½ onion, finely chopped
2 garlic cloves, crushed
300ml/½ pint/1¼ cups chicken stock
3.5ml/¾ tsp dried thyme
2.5ml/½ tsp dried basil
30ml/2 tbsp finely chopped fresh parsley
30ml/2 tbsp lemon juice
mint leaves, to garnish

1 Preheat the oven to 180°C/350°F/Gas 4. Cook the sweet potato in boiling water until tender, drain, transfer to a bowl and mash. Add the onion, tarragon, basil, chilli, garlic, thyme and prawns, season with pepper and mix well.

2 Lay the turkey fillets on a plate and season. Place a little of the sweet potato stuffing in the centre of each, fold over the sides and roll up. Secure with a cocktail stick or toothpick, and place in a buttered ovenproof dish, seam-side down.

3 To make the sauce, heat the oil in a frying pan and fry the onion and garlic for 5–7 minutes until soft. Stir in the stock and simmer briefly. Add the herbs and lemon juice, and simmer for 2 minutes. Season to taste.

4 Pour the sauce around the turkey, cover with foil and bake for 1½ hours, basting frequently with the sauce to keep the rolls moist. Garnish with mint and serve with bulgur wheat or rice.

Duck with Sherry & Pumpkin

For this dish, duck is marinated in a mixture of spices and cooked in a smooth pumpkin and tomato sauce enriched with medium-dry sherry.

Serves 6

1 whole duck, about 1.75kg/3lb
1 lemon
5ml/1 tsp garlic granules or 2 garlic cloves, crushed
5ml/1 tsp curry powder
2.5ml/½ tsp paprika

3.5ml/¾ tsp Indian five-spice powder
30ml/2 tbsp soy sauce, plus extra to serve
vegetable oil, for frying
salt and freshly ground black pepper

For the sauce

75g/3oz pumpkin
1 onion, chopped
4 canned plum tomatoes
300ml/½ pint/1¼ cups medium-dry sherry
about 300ml/½ pint/1¼ cups water

1 Cut the duck into 10 pieces and place in a large bowl. Halve the lemon and squeeze the juice all over the duck. Set aside.

2 In a small bowl, mix together the garlic, curry powder, paprika, five-spice powder and salt and pepper, and rub well into the duck pieces. Sprinkle the duck with the soy sauce, cover loosely with clear film (plastic wrap) and set aside to marinate overnight.

3 To make the sauce, cook the pumpkin in boiling water until tender. Blend to a purée with the onion and tomatoes in a food processor or blender.

4 Pat the duck pieces dry with kitchen paper. Heat a little oil in a wok or large frying pan and fry the duck for 15 minutes until crisp and brown. Remove from the pan and set aside.

5 Wipe away the excess oil from the wok or frying pan with kitchen paper and pour in the pumpkin purée. Add the sherry and a little of the water, then bring to the boil and add the fried duck. Simmer for about 1 hour until the duck is cooked, adding more water if the sauce becomes too thick. Serve hot and hand soy sauce separately.

Hot Chilli Duck with Crab Meat & Cashew Nut Sauce

Perhaps a surprising partner for duck, crab meat nonetheless makes a wonderful rich sauce with Thai spices and coconut.

Serves 4–6

2.75kg/6lb duck
about 1.2 litres/2 pints/5 cups water
2 kaffir lime leaves
2–3 small fresh red chillies, seeded and finely chopped
25ml/5 tsp sugar
30ml/2 tbsp coriander seeds
5ml/1 tsp caraway seeds
115g/4oz/1 cup cashew nuts, chopped
7.5cm/3in piece lemon grass, shredded
2.5cm/1in piece galangal or fresh root ginger, finely chopped
2 garlic cloves, crushed
4 shallots or 1 medium onion, finely chopped
2cm/¾in cube shrimp paste
25g/1oz/½ cup coriander (cilantro) white root or stem, finely chopped
175g/6oz frozen white crab meat, thawed
50g/2oz creamed coconut (coconut cream)
salt
1 small bunch fresh coriander (cilantro), chopped, to garnish
cooked Thai fragrant rice, to serve

1 To portion the duck into manageable pieces, first remove the legs. Separate the thighs from the drumsticks and chop each thigh and drumstick into 2 pieces. Trim away the lower half of the duck with kitchen scissors. Cut the breast piece in half down the middle, then chop each half into 4 pieces.

2 Put the duck flesh and bones into a large heavy pan and add the water – it should just cover the meat. Add the lime leaves and 5ml/1 tsp salt, bring to the boil and simmer, uncovered, for 35–40 minutes until the duck is tender. Discard the bones, skim off the fat from the stock and place in a clean pan.

3 Grind the chillies together with the sugar and 2.5ml/½ tsp salt using a food processor. Dry-fry the coriander and caraway seeds and the cashews in a wok for about 1–2 minutes. Add to the food processor with the lemon grass, galangal or ginger, garlic and shallots or onion and process to a smooth paste. Add the shrimp paste and coriander root or stem.

4 Add 250ml/8fl oz/1 cup of the duck stock to the spicy mixture in the food processor and blend to make a thin paste. Pour the spice paste in with the duck, bring to the boil and simmer, uncovered, for 20–25 minutes.

5 Add the crab meat and creamed coconut, and simmer briefly. Turn out on to a serving dish, garnish with chopped coriander and serve, accompanied by Thai fragrant rice.

> **Cook's Tip**
> *Shrimp paste is made from dried shrimp fermented in brine. It both smells and tastes strongly, so add it with caution. It is used widely throughout South-east Asia, where it is known as blacan or blachan. The Japanese variety is called terasi.*

Hot Sweet-&-Sour Duck Casserole

This dish has a distinctively sweet, sour and hot flavour, and is best eaten with rice as an accompaniment.

Serves 4–6

1.3kg/3lb duck, jointed and skinned
4 bay leaves
45ml/3 tbsp salt
75ml/5 tbsp vegetable oil
juice of 5 lemons
8 medium onions, finely chopped
50g/2oz garlic, crushed
50g/2oz chilli powder
300ml/½ pint/1¼ cups pickling vinegar
115g/4oz fresh root ginger, thinly sliced or shredded
115g/4oz/generous ½ cup sugar
50g/2oz garam masala

1 Place the duck, bay leaves and salt in a large pan and cover with cold water. Bring to the boil, then simmer until the duck is fully cooked: the juices should run clear when the thickest part of the thigh is pierced with a skewer or knife. Remove the duck from the pan and keep warm. Reserve the liquid to use as a base for stock or soups.

2 In a large pan, heat the oil and lemon juice until it reaches smoking point. Add the onions, garlic and chilli powder, and fry until the onions are golden brown.

3 Add the vinegar, ginger and sugar, and simmer until the sugar dissolves and the oil has separated.

4 Add the duck to the pan with the garam masala. Mix well, then reheat until the masala clings to the pieces of duck and the gravy is thick. Taste and adjust the seasoning as necessary. If you prefer a thinner gravy, add a little of the reserved stock. Serve hot.

> **Variation**
> *This recipe also works well with most game birds. Try it with guinea fowl, pheasant or partridge – or, of course, wild duck, such as teal or widgeon.*

FIERY CHICKEN CURRIES

Recent research has suggested something that curry lovers have known for years – curry is addictive and makes people feel good. If that proves to be true, be prepared for complete delirium with this sizzling collection of Indian, Balti, Thai and other curries. The secret of preparing an authentic curry, whatever its nationality, is not simply making it hot – some are quite mild – but lies in the careful balance of the spices. Indian cooks all mix their own garam masala, and their Thai counterparts are equally fussy with their red and green curry pastes. All the recipes in this chapter reflect this concern with subtle spicing, although that doesn't mean that fiercely hot curries are not included. Balti Chicken Vindaloo and Hot Chilli Chicken, for example, are not for the faint-hearted. The recipes range from mellow, rich and creamy at one end of the scale to truly mouth-scorching at the other. In between, there are fragrant and sweet-and-sour curries, as well as some that are just pleasantly hot. The selection of other ingredients is almost as important as the choice of spices, and the recipes in this chapter include a wide range – lentils, coconut, mint, tomatoes, potatoes and even apples are used to delight the palate.

Chicken in a Cashew Nut Sauce

This chicken dish has a deliciously thick and nutty sauce, and it is best served with plain boiled rice.

Serves 4
2 medium onions
30ml/2 tbsp tomato
   purée (paste)
50g/2oz/ ½ cup cashew nuts
7.5ml/1½ tsp garam masala
5ml/1 tsp crushed garlic
5ml/1 tsp chilli powder
15ml/1 tbsp lemon juice

1.5ml/ ¼ tsp ground turmeric
5ml/1 tsp salt
15ml/1 tbsp natural (plain) low-
   fat yogurt
15ml/1 tbsp corn oil
30ml/2 tbsp chopped
   fresh coriander (cilantro)
15ml/1 tbsp sultanas
   (golden raisins)
450g/1lb skinless boneless
   chicken, cubed
175g/6oz/2½ cups button
   (white) mushrooms
300ml/ ½ pint/1¼ cups water

1 Cut the onions into quarters, place in a food processor or blender and process for about 1 minute. Pour off any liquid that has accumulated in the bowl of the processor.

2 Add the tomato purée (paste), cashew nuts, garam masala, garlic, chilli powder, lemon juice, turmeric, salt and yogurt to the onions. Process for a further 1–1½ minutes.

3 In a heavy pan, heat the corn oil, lower the heat to medium and pour in the spice mixture from the food processor, scraping out the contents with a firm spatula. Fry for about 2 minutes, lowering the heat if necessary.

4 Add half the chopped coriander, the sultanas and chicken, and continue to stir-fry for a further 1 minute.

5 Add the mushrooms, pour in the water and bring to a simmer. Cover the pan and cook over a low heat for about 10 minutes.

6 Check if the chicken is cooked through and the sauce is thick. Cook for a little longer if necessary. Serve, garnished with the remaining chopped fresh coriander.

Fragrant Chicken Curry

In this dish, the mildly spiced sauce is thickened using lentils rather than the traditional onions fried in ghee.

Serves 4
75g/3oz/ ⅓ cup red lentils
30ml/2 tbsp mild curry powder
10ml/2 tsp ground coriander
5ml/1 tsp cumin seeds
475ml/16fl oz/2 cups
   vegetable stock

8 skinless chicken thighs, skinned
225g/8oz fresh spinach, shredded
   or frozen spinach, thawed and
   well drained
15ml/1 tbsp chopped
   fresh coriander (cilantro)
salt and freshly ground
   black pepper
fresh coriander (cilantro),
   to garnish
boiled white or brown basmati
   rice and grilled (broiled)
   poppadums, to serve

1 Rinse the lentils under cold running water. Put into a large, heavy pan with the curry powder, ground coriander, cumin seeds and stock.

2 Bring to the boil, then lower the heat. Cover and simmer gently for 10 minutes.

3 Add the chicken and spinach to the lentils. Re-cover and simmer gently for a further 40 minutes or until the chicken is cooked through and tender.

4 Stir in the chopped fresh coriander and season to taste. Serve, garnished with fresh coriander sprigs, accompanied by rice and grilled poppadums.

Chicken Korma

A korma is a rich, creamy Moghulai dish that originates from northern India. This recipe uses a combination of yogurt and cream which gives the sauce a delicious, subtle flavour.

Serves 4

675g/1½lb skinless chicken breast fillets
25g/1oz/¼ cup blanched almonds
2 garlic cloves, crushed
2.5cm/1in piece fresh root ginger, roughly chopped
30ml/2 tbsp oil
3 green cardamom pods
1 onion, finely chopped
10ml/2 tsp ground cumin
1.5ml/¼ tsp salt
150ml/¼ pint/⅔ cup natural (plain) yogurt
175ml/6fl oz/¾ cup single (light) cream
toasted flaked (sliced) almonds and fresh coriander (cilantro), to garnish
boiled rice, to serve

1 Cut the chicken fillets into 2.5cm/1in cubes. Put the blanched almonds, crushed garlic and ginger into a food processor or blender with 30ml/2 tbsp water, and process to a smooth paste, pushing down the contents once with a spatula.

2 Heat the oil in a large frying pan and fry the chicken for 8–10 minutes or until browned. Remove using a slotted spoon and set aside.

3 Add the cardamom pods to the pan and fry for 2 minutes. Add the onion and fry for a further 5 minutes. Stir in the almond and garlic paste, cumin and salt and cook, stirring constantly, for a further 5 minutes.

4 Add the yogurt, a tablespoonful at a time, and cook over a low heat, until it has all been absorbed. Return the chicken to the pan. Cover and simmer over a low heat for 5–6 minutes or until the chicken is tender.

5 Add the cream and simmer for a further 5 minutes. Serve with boiled rice and garnish with toasted flaked almonds and fresh coriander.

Simple Chicken Curry

Curry powder can be bought in three different strengths – mild, medium and hot. Use the type you prefer to suit your taste.

Serves 4

8 chicken legs (thighs and drumsticks)
30ml/2 tbsp olive oil
1 onion, thinly sliced
1 garlic clove, crushed
15ml/1 tbsp medium curry powder
15ml/1 tbsp plain (all-purpose) flour
450ml/¾ pint/scant 2 cups chicken stock
1 beefsteak tomato
15ml/1 tbsp mango chutney
15ml/1 tbsp lemon juice
salt and freshly ground black pepper
boiled rice, to serve

1 Cut the chicken legs in half. Heat the oil in a large, flameproof casserole and brown the chicken on all sides. Remove from the casserole and keep warm.

2 Add the onion and garlic to the casserole and cook over a fairly low heat until tender. Add the curry powder and cook gently for 2 minutes, stirring constantly.

3 Stir in the flour and gradually blend in the stock. Season to taste with salt and pepper. Bring to the boil, return the chicken pieces to the casserole, cover and simmer for 20–30 minutes or until tender.

4 Peel the tomato by blanching in boiling water for 15 seconds, then plunging into cold water to loosen the skin. Peel and cut into small cubes, discarding the seeds.

5 Add the tomato to the chicken with the mango chutney and lemon juice. Heat through gently and adjust the seasoning to taste. Serve with plenty of boiled rice.

Moghul-style Chicken

This delicate curry can be served as an appetizer followed by stronger curries and rice. Saffron is a crucial ingredient, but as it is very expensive, save the dish for special occasions.

Serves 4–6

4 chicken breast portions, rubbed
   with a little garam masala
2 eggs, beaten with salt
   and pepper
90ml/6 tbsp ghee or
   melted butter
1 large onion, finely chopped

5cm/2in piece fresh root
   ginger, crushed
4 garlic cloves, crushed
4 cloves
4 green cardamoms
5cm/2in cinnamon stick
2 bay leaves
15–20 saffron threads
150ml/ ¼ pint/ ⅔ cup natural
   (plain) yogurt, beaten with 5ml/
   1 tsp cornflour (cornstarch)
salt
75ml/5 tbsp double
   (heavy) cream
50g/2oz/ ½ cup ground almonds

1 Brush the chicken breast portions with the beaten eggs. Heat the ghee or butter in a frying pan and fry the chicken. Remove from the pan and keep warm.

2 In the remaining fat, fry the finely chopped onion, crushed ginger, garlic, cloves, green cardamoms, cinnamon stick and bay leaves. When the onion turns golden brown, remove the pan from the heat, set aside to cool a little, then stir in the saffron and yogurt.

3 Return the chicken to the pan with any juices and cook over a low heat until the chicken is tender. Taste and adjust the seasoning as necessary. Just before serving, fold in the cream and ground almonds. Serve hot.

> **Cook's Tip**
> If you don't have time to make your own ghee, clarified butter and vegetable ghee are available from Indian foodstores and supermarkets.

Special Chicken Curry

Chicken curry is always popular when served at a family dinner. This version is cooked covered, giving a thin consistency. If you like it thicker, cook uncovered for the last 15 minutes.

Serves 4–6

60ml/4 tbsp vegetable oil
4 cloves
4–6 green cardamoms
5cm/2in cinnamon stick
3 whole star anise
6–8 curry leaves
1 large onion, finely chopped

5cm/2in piece fresh root
   ginger, crushed
4 garlic cloves, crushed
60ml/4 tbsp mild curry paste
5ml/1 tsp ground turmeric
5ml/1 tsp five-spice powder
1.3kg/3lb chicken, skinned
   and jointed
400g/14oz can
   chopped tomatoes
115g/4oz block creamed coconut
   (coconut cream)
2.5ml/ ½ tsp sugar
50g/2oz/1 cup fresh
   coriander (cilantro), chopped
salt

1 Heat the oil in a frying pan and fry the cloves, cardamoms, cinnamon stick, star anise and curry leaves until the cloves swell and the curry leaves are slightly burnt.

2 Add the onion, ginger and garlic, and fry until the onion turns brown. Add the curry paste, turmeric and five-spice powder, and fry until the oil separates.

3 Add the chicken pieces and mix well. When all the pieces are evenly sealed, cover and cook until the meat is nearly done.

4 Add the chopped tomatoes and the creamed coconut. Simmer gently until the coconut dissolves. Mix well, add the sugar and salt to taste. Fold in the coriander leaves, reheat gently and serve hot.

> **Cook's Tip**
> Indian five-spice powder is different from Chinese. Make sure you buy the Indian variety for this dish.

Kashmiri Chicken Curry

This mild yet flavoursome dish is given a special lift by the addition of apples.

Serves 4

10ml/2 tsp corn oil
2 medium onions, diced
1 bay leaf
2 cloves
2.5cm/1in cinnamon stick
4 black peppercorns
1 baby chicken, about 675g/ 1½ lb skinned and cut into 8 pieces
5ml/1 tsp garam masala
5ml/1 tsp grated fresh root ginger
5ml/1 tsp crushed garlic
5ml/1 tsp salt
5ml/1 tsp chilli powder
15ml/1 tbsp ground almonds
150ml/¼ pint/⅔ cup natural (plain) low-fat yogurt
2 green eating apples, peeled, cored and roughly sliced
15ml/1 tbsp chopped fresh coriander (cilantro)
15g/½ oz flaked (sliced) almonds, lightly toasted, and fresh coriander (cilantro) leaves, to garnish

1 Heat the oil in a non-stick wok or frying pan and fry the onions with the bay leaf, cloves, cinnamon and peppercorns for about 3–5 minutes. Add the chicken pieces and continue to stir-fry for at least 3 minutes.

2 Lower the heat and add the garam masala, ginger, garlic, salt, chilli powder and ground almonds, and continue to stir for 2–3 minutes. Pour in the yogurt and stir over a low heat for a further 2–3 minutes. Add the apples and chopped coriander, cover and cook for about 10–15 minutes.

3 Check that the chicken is cooked through, and serve immediately, garnished with toasted flaked almonds and whole coriander leaves.

Cook's Tip
While less fat may be required, a wok with a non-stick lining cannot be heated to high temperatures. A well-seasoned cast-iron wok also works in a "non-stick" way.

Karahi Chicken with Mint

For this tasty dish, the chicken is first boiled before being quickly stir-fried in a little oil, to ensure that it is cooked through despite the short cooking time.

Serves 4

275g/10oz skinless chicken breast fillet, cut into strips
300ml/½ pint/1¼ cups water
15ml/1 tbsp soya oil
2 small bunches spring onions (scallions), roughly chopped
5ml/1 tsp grated fresh root ginger
5ml/1 tsp crushed dried red chillies
30ml/2 tbsp lemon juice
15ml/1 tbsp chopped fresh coriander (cilantro)
15ml/1 tbsp chopped fresh mint
3 tomatoes, seeded and roughly chopped
5ml/1 tsp salt
fresh mint and coriander (cilantro) sprigs, to garnish

1 Put the chicken and water into a pan, bring to the boil and lower the heat to medium. Cook for about 10 minutes or until the water has evaporated and the chicken is cooked. Remove from the heat and set aside.

2 Heat the soya oil in a heavy non-stick frying pan or other suitable pan and add the spring onions. Stir-fry over a medium heat for about 2 minutes until soft and translucent. Add the boiled chicken strips and stir-fry over a medium heat for a further 3 minutes.

3 Gradually add the ginger, dried chillies, lemon juice, coriander, mint, tomatoes and salt and stir for a few minutes to blend all the flavours together. Transfer to a serving dish, garnish with mint and coriander sprigs, and serve immediately.

Cook's Tip
If fresh mint is not available, use a jar of mint that has been shredded and preserved in salt and vinegar, rather than the dried herb. The opened jar should be stored in the refrigerator.

Chicken Tikka

The red food colouring gives this dish its traditional bright colour. Serve with lemon wedges.

Serves 4
1.5kg/3½ lb chicken
mixed salad leaves, e.g. frisée and
   oakleaf lettuce or radicchio, and
   lemon wedges, to serve

For the marinade
150ml/ ¼ pint/ ⅔ cup natural
   (plain) low-fat yogurt
5ml/1 tsp paprika
10ml/2 tsp grated fresh
   root ginger
1 garlic clove, crushed
10ml/2 tsp garam masala
2.5ml/ ½ tsp salt
red food colouring (optional)
juice of 1 lemon

1 Joint the chicken and cut it into 8 pieces, using a sharp knife.

2 To make the marinade, mix all the ingredients in a large dish. Add the chicken pieces and turn to coat them thoroughly. Chill for 4 hours or overnight in the refrigerator to allow the flavours to penetrate the flesh.

3 Preheat the oven to 200°C/400°F/Gas 6. Remove the chicken pieces from the marinade using a slotted spoon and arrange them in a single layer in a large, ovenproof dish. Bake for 30–40 minutes or until tender, basting with a little of the marinade while cooking.

4 Arrange the chicken on a bed of salad leaves and serve hot or cold with lemon wedges for squeezing.

Cook's Tip
Poppadums can be a healthy accompaniment to a low-fat Indian meal. Instead of frying them, put them, one at a time, on the turntable of a microwave oven and cook on HIGH for 40–60 seconds. They will not be quite so puffed up as fried poppadums, but will still be crisp – and much healthier.

Tandoori Chicken

Although the authentic tandoori flavour is very difficult to achieve in conventional ovens, this low-fat version still makes a very tasty dish.

Serves 4
4 chicken quarters
175ml/6fl oz/ ¾ cup natural
   (plain) low-fat yogurt
5ml/1 tsp garam masala
5ml/1 tsp grated fresh root ginger

5ml/1 tsp crushed garlic
7.5ml/1½ tsp chilli powder
1.5ml/ ¼ tsp ground turmeric
5ml/1 tsp ground coriander
15ml/1 tbsp lemon juice
5ml/1 tsp salt
a few drops of red food colouring
15ml/1 tbsp corn oil

For the garnish
mixed salad leaves
lime wedges

1 Skin and rinse the chicken quarters, then pat dry with kitchen paper. Make 2 slits into the flesh of each piece, place in a dish and set aside.

2 In a bowl, mix together the yogurt, garam masala, ginger, garlic, chilli powder, turmeric, coriander, lemon juice, salt, red food colouring and oil. Beat well so that all the ingredients are thoroughly combined.

3 Cover the chicken quarters with the yogurt and spice mixture, turning them to coat well and set aside to marinate for about 3 hours.

4 Preheat the oven to 240°C/475°F/Gas 9. Transfer the chicken pieces to an ovenproof dish. Bake for about 20–25 minutes or until the chicken is cooked right through, browned on top and the juices run clear when the thickest part is pierced with a skewer or the point of a knife.

5 Remove from the oven and transfer to a serving dish. Garnish with the salad leaves and lime, and serve.

Chicken Saag

A mildly spiced dish using a popular combination of spinach and chicken. It is best made using fresh spinach, but if this is unavailable, you can substitute frozen. Do not use canned.

Serves 4

225g/8oz spinach leaves, washed but not dried
2.5cm/1in piece fresh root ginger, grated
2 garlic cloves, crushed
1 fresh green chilli, roughly chopped
200ml/7fl oz/scant 1 cup water
30ml/2 tbsp vegetable oil
2 bay leaves
1.5ml/¼ tsp black peppercorns
1 onion, finely chopped
4 tomatoes, peeled and finely chopped
10ml/2 tsp curry powder
5ml/1 tsp salt
5ml/1 tsp chilli powder
45ml/3 tbsp natural (plain) yogurt
8 skinless chicken thighs
natural (plain) yogurt and chilli powder, to garnish
masala naan bread, to serve

1 Cook the spinach, without water, in a tightly covered pan for 5 minutes. Put the spinach, ginger, garlic and chilli with 50ml/2fl oz/¼ cup of the water into a food processor or blender, and process to a thick purée.

2 Heat the oil in a large pan, add the bay leaves and peppercorns and fry for 2 minutes. Add the onion and fry for 6–8 minutes or until the onion has browned.

3 Add the tomatoes and simmer for about 5 minutes. Stir in the curry powder, salt and chilli powder, and cook for 2 minutes.

4 Add the spinach purée and the remaining water and simmer for 5 minutes. Add the yogurt, a tablespoonful at a time, and simmer for 5 minutes.

5 Add the chicken. Cover and cook for 25–30 minutes or until the chicken is tender. Serve on masala naan bread, drizzle over some yogurt and dust with chilli powder.

Chicken Dhansak

Dhansak curries originate from the Parsee community and are traditionally made with lentils and meat.

Serves 4

75g/3oz/scant ½ cup green lentils
475ml/16fl oz/2 cups chicken stock
45ml/3 tbsp vegetable oil
5ml/1 tsp cumin seeds
2 curry leaves
1 onion, finely chopped
2.5cm/1in piece fresh root ginger, chopped
1 fresh green chilli, finely chopped
5ml/1 tsp ground cumin
5ml/1 tsp ground coriander
1.5ml/¼ tsp salt
1.5ml/¼ tsp chilli powder
400g/14oz can chopped tomatoes
8 skinless chicken portions
60ml/4 tbsp chopped fresh coriander (cilantro)
5ml/1 tsp garam masala
fresh coriander (cilantro) sprigs, to garnish
cooked plain and yellow rice, to serve

1 Rinse the lentils under cold running water. Put them into a large, heavy pan with the stock. Bring to the boil, lower the heat, cover and simmer for about 15–20 minutes. Set aside without draining.

2 Heat the oil in a large pan and fry the cumin seeds and curry leaves for 2 minutes. Add the onion, ginger and chilli and fry for about 5 minutes. Stir in the cumin, coriander, salt and chilli powder with 30ml/2 tbsp water.

3 Add the tomatoes and chicken. Cover and cook over a medium heat for 10–15 minutes.

4 Add the lentils and their stock, the fresh coriander and the garam masala, and cook for 10 minutes or until the chicken is tender. Garnish with coriander sprigs and serve immediately with plain and yellow rice.

Chicken with Mild Balti Spices

This recipe has a beautifully delicate flavour and is probably the most popular of all Balti dishes.

Serves 4–6
45ml/3 tbsp corn oil
3 medium onions, sliced
3 medium tomatoes, halved
   and sliced
2.5cm/1in cinnamon stick
2 large black cardamom pods
4 black peppercorns

2.5ml/½ tsp black cumin seeds
5ml/1 tsp grated fresh root ginger
5ml/1 tsp crushed garlic
5ml/1 tsp garam masala
5ml/1 tsp chilli powder
5ml/1 tsp salt
1.3kg/3lb chicken, skinned and
   cut into 8 pieces
30ml/2 tbsp natural (plain) yogurt
60ml/4 tbsp lemon juice
30ml/2 tbsp chopped
   fresh coriander (cilantro)
2 fresh green chillies, chopped

1 Heat the oil in a wok or heavy frying pan. Add the onions and fry until they are golden brown. Add the tomatoes and stir well. Add the cinnamon stick, cardamoms, peppercorns, black cumin seeds, ginger, garlic, garam masala, chilli powder and salt. Lower the heat and stir-fry for 3–5 minutes.

2 Add the chicken pieces, 2 at a time, and stir-fry for at least 7 minutes or until the spice mixture has completely penetrated the chicken. Add the yogurt and mix well.

3 Lower the heat and cover the pan with a piece of foil, making sure that the foil does not touch the food. Cook very gently for about 15 minutes, checking once to make sure the sauce is not catching on the base of the pan. Finally, add the lemon juice, fresh coriander and green chillies, and serve at once.

Cook's Tip
Chicken cooked on the bone is both tender and flavoursome. However, you can substitute the whole chicken with 675g/1½lb boned and cubed chicken, if wished. The cooking time can be reduced in step 3 too.

Balti Butter Chicken

Another favourite mild Balti dish, especially in the West. Cooked in butter, with aromatic spices, cream and almonds, it will be enjoyed by everyone.

Serves 4–6
150ml/¼ pint/⅔ cup natural
   (plain) yogurt
50g/2oz/½ cup ground almonds
7.5ml/1½ tsp chilli powder
1.5ml/¼ tsp crushed bay leaves
1.5ml/¼ tsp ground cloves
1.5ml/¼ tsp ground cinnamon
5ml/1 tsp garam masala

4 green cardamom pods
5ml/1 tsp grated fresh root ginger
5ml/1 tsp crushed garlic
400g/14oz can tomatoes
5ml/1 tsp salt
1kg/2¼lb chicken, skinned, boned
   and cubed
75g/3oz/6 tbsp butter
15ml/1 tbsp corn oil
2 medium onions, sliced
30ml/2 tbsp chopped
   fresh coriander (cilantro)
60ml/4 tbsp single (light) cream
fresh coriander (cilantro) sprigs,
   to garnish

1 Put the yogurt, ground almonds, all the dry spices, the ginger, garlic, tomatoes and salt into a bowl, and blend together.

2 Place the chicken in a large bowl and pour over the yogurt mixture, turning to coat. Set aside.

3 Heat the butter and oil in a medium karahi or deep, round-based frying pan. Add the onions and fry for about 3 minutes.

4 Add the chicken mixture and stir-fry for 7–10 minutes. Stir in about half of the coriander and mix well.

5 Pour over the cream and stir in well. Bring to the boil. Sprinkle with the remaining chopped coriander, garnish with fresh coriander sprigs and serve.

Cook's Tip
Substitute the natural yogurt with Greek (US strained plain) yogurt for an even richer and creamier flavour.

Jeera Chicken

An aromatic dish with a delicious, distinctive taste of cumin. Serve simply with a cooling cucumber raita.

Serves 4
45ml/3 tbsp cumin seeds
45ml/3 tbsp oil
2.5ml/ ½ tsp black peppercorns
4 green cardamom pods
2 fresh green chillies,
  finely chopped
2 garlic cloves, crushed
2.5cm/1in piece fresh root
  ginger, grated
5ml/1 tsp ground coriander
10ml/2 tsp ground cumin
2.5ml/ ½ tsp salt
8 skinless chicken portions, e.g.
  thighs and drumsticks
5ml/1 tsp garam masala
fresh coriander (cilantro) and chilli
  powder, to garnish
cucumber raita, to serve

1 Dry-fry 15ml/1 tbsp of the cumin seeds in a heavy frying pan for 5 minutes. Remove from the heat and set aside.

2 Heat the oil in a large pan and fry the remaining cumin seeds, peppercorns and cardamoms for 2–3 minutes. Add the chillies, garlic and ginger, and fry for 2 minutes. Add the ground coriander, cumin and salt, and cook for 2–3 minutes. Add the chicken. Cover and simmer for 20–25 minutes.

3 Add the garam masala and toasted cumin seeds, and cook for a further 5 minutes. Serve with cucumber raita, garnished with chilli powder and fresh coriander.

> **Cook's Tip**
> *Raitas are very easy to make. For a cucumber raita, mix together 300ml/½ pint/1¼ cups lightly beaten natural (plain) yogurt, ½ diced cucumber and 1 seeded and chopped fresh green chilli. Season with salt and a pinch of ground cumin. Cover and chill before serving. For a tomato raita, mix the yogurt with 2 peeled, seeded and finely chopped tomatoes, season with salt and stir in 15ml/1 tbsp chopped fresh coriander (cilantro).*

Chicken in a Spicy Yogurt Marinade

Plan this dish well in advance; the extra-long marinating time is necessary to develop a really mellow, spicy flavour.

Serves 6
6 chicken portions
juice of 1 lemon
5ml/1 tsp salt
salad leaves and lemon or lime
  slices, to serve

For the marinade
5ml/1 tsp coriander seeds
10ml/2 tsp cumin seeds
6 cloves
2 bay leaves
1 onion, quartered
2 garlic cloves
5cm/2in piece fresh root ginger,
  roughly chopped
2.5ml/ ½ tsp chilli powder
5ml/1 tsp ground turmeric
150ml/ ¼ pint/ ⅔ cup natural
  (plain) yogurt

1 Skin the chicken portions and make deep slashes in the fleshiest parts with a sharp knife. Place in a non-metallic dish, sprinkle the lemon juice and salt over them and rub in with your fingertips. Set aside.

2 Spread the coriander and cumin seeds, cloves and bay leaves in the base of a large frying pan and dry-fry over a moderate heat until the bay leaves are crispy.

3 Set the spices aside to cool, then grind coarsely using a pestle and mortar or spice grinder.

4 Mince (grind) the onion, garlic and ginger in a food processor or blender. Add the ground spices, the chilli powder, turmeric and yogurt, then strain in the lemon juice from the chicken.

5 Arrange the chicken in a single layer in a roasting pan. Pour over the spice mixture, then cover and marinate for 24–36 hours in the refrigerator. Turn the chicken pieces occasionally in the marinade.

6 Preheat the oven to 200°C/400°F/Gas 6. Cook the chicken for 45 minutes. Serve hot or cold, with salad leaves and slices of lemon or lime.

Balti Chicken in a Thick Creamy Coconut Sauce

If you like the flavour of coconut, you will really love this curry, which contains both desiccated coconut and coconut milk.

Serves 4

15ml/1 tbsp ground almonds
15ml/1 tbsp desiccated
  (dry, unsweetened
  shredded) coconut
90ml/6 tbsp coconut milk
175g/6oz/¾ cup fromage frais
  (cream cheese)
7.5ml/1½ tsp ground coriander
5ml/1 tsp chilli powder
5ml/1 tsp crushed garlic
7.5ml/1½ tsp grated fresh
  root ginger
5ml/1 tsp salt
15ml/1 tbsp corn oil
225g/8oz skinless, boneless
  chicken, cubed
3 green cardamom pods
1 bay leaf
1 dried red chilli, crushed
30ml/2 tbsp chopped
  fresh coriander (cilantro)

1 Dry-fry the ground almonds and desiccated coconut in a heavy pan until they turn a shade darker. Transfer to a mixing bowl. Add the coconut milk, fromage frais, ground coriander, chilli powder, garlic, ginger and salt.

2 Heat the oil in a non-stick wok or frying pan and add the chicken cubes, cardamoms and bay leaf. Stir-fry for about 2 minutes to seal the chicken.

3 Pour in the coconut milk mixture and blend everything together. Lower the heat, add the crushed dried chilli and fresh coriander, cover and cook for 10–12 minutes, stirring occasionally. Uncover, then stir and cook for a further 2 minutes before serving.

> **Cook's Tip**
> *Cut the chicken into small, equal-size cubes for speedy and even cooking.*

Balti Chicken in Hara Masala Sauce

A little fresh and dried fruit with mint and coriander leaves and spring onions flavour the creamy sauce of this dish.

Serves 4

1 crisp green eating apple,
  peeled, cored and cut into
  small cubes
60ml/4 tbsp fresh coriander
  (cilantro) leaves
30ml/2 tbsp fresh mint leaves
120ml/4fl oz/½ cup natural
  (plain) yogurt
45ml/3 tbsp fromage frais
  (cream cheese)
2 medium fresh green chillies,
  seeded and chopped
1 bunch spring onions
  (scallions), chopped
5ml/1 tsp salt
5ml/1 tsp sugar
5ml/1 tsp crushed garlic
5ml/1 tsp grated fresh root ginger
15ml/1 tbsp corn oil
225g/8oz skinless chicken breast
  fillets, cubed
25g/1oz/¼ cup sultanas
  (golden raisins)

1 Place the eating apple, 45ml/3 tbsp of the coriander, half the mint, the yogurt, fromage frais, chillies, spring onions, salt, sugar, garlic and ginger in a food processor and pulse for about 1 minute.

2 Heat the oil in a non-stick wok or frying pan, pour in the yogurt mixture and cook over a low heat for about 2 minutes.

3 Add the chicken pieces and blend everything together. Cook over a medium-low heat for 12–15 minutes or until the chicken is fully cooked.

4 Finally, add the sultanas and the remaining coriander and mint leaves, and serve immediately.

> **Cook's Tip**
> *This dish makes a good dinner-party centrepiece.*

Chicken & Tomato Balti

If you like tomatoes, you will love this chicken recipe. It makes a semi-dry Balti, and is good served with a lentil dish and plain boiled rice.

Serves 4
60ml/4 tbsp corn oil
6 curry leaves
2.5ml/ ½ tsp mixed onion and mustard seeds
8 medium tomatoes, sliced

5ml/1 tsp ground coriander
5ml/1 tsp chilli powder
5ml/1 tsp salt
5ml/1 tsp ground cumin
5ml/1 tsp crushed garlic
675g/1½lb skinless, boneless chicken, cubed
150ml/ ¼ pint/ ⅔ cup water
15ml/1 tbsp sesame seeds, roasted
15ml/1 tbsp chopped fresh coriander (cilantro)

1 Heat the oil in a medium karahi or a deep, round-based frying pan. Add the curry leaves and mixed onion and mustard seeds and stir thoroughly. Lower the heat slightly and add the sliced tomatoes.

2 While the tomatoes are gently cooking, mix together the ground coriander, chilli powder, salt, ground cumin and garlic in a bowl. Tip the spices on to the tomatoes.

3 Add the chicken pieces and mix together well. Stir-fry for about 5 minutes.

4 Pour in the water and continue cooking, stirring occasionally, until the sauce thickens and the chicken is cooked through.

5 Sprinkle the sesame seeds and fresh coriander over the top of the dish and serve.

Cook's Tip
Although it takes very little time to roast sesame seeds, you may find it more convenient to buy them ready-roasted from an Indian foodstore.

Khara Masala Balti Chicken

Whole spices *(khara)* are used in this recipe, giving it a wonderfully rich flavour. This is a dry dish so it is best served with a refreshing raita and paratha.

Serves 4
3 curry leaves
1.5ml/ ¼ tsp mustard seeds
1.5ml/ ¼ tsp fennel seeds
1.5ml/ ¼ tsp onion seeds
2.5ml/ ½ tsp crushed dried red chillies
2.5ml/ ½ tsp white cumin seeds

1.5ml/ ¼ tsp fenugreek seeds
2.5ml/ ½ tsp crushed pomegranate seeds
5ml/1 tsp salt
5ml/1 tsp grated fresh root ginger
3 garlic cloves, sliced
60ml/4 tbsp corn oil
4 fresh green chillies, slit
1 large onion, sliced
1 medium tomato, sliced
675g/1½lb skinless, boneless chicken, cubed
15ml/1 tbsp chopped fresh coriander (cilantro)

1 Mix together the curry leaves, mustard seeds, fennel seeds, onion seeds, crushed red chillies, cumin seeds, fenugreek seeds, crushed pomegranate seeds and salt in a large bowl. Add the ginger and garlic.

2 Heat the oil in a medium karahi or deep round-based frying pan. Add the spice mixture, then the green chillies. Add the onion and stir-fry over a medium heat for 5–7 minutes.

3 Add the tomato and chicken pieces, and cook over a medium heat for about 7 minutes. The chicken should be cooked through and the sauce reduced.

4 Stir over a medium heat for a further 3–5 minutes, then serve hot, garnished with chopped fresh coriander.

Cook's Tip
Paratha is unleavened bread with a flaky texture rather like chapati. It is available from Indian foodstores.

Chicken Tikka Masala

Tender chicken pieces cooked in a creamy, spicy sauce with a hint of tomato and served on naan bread.

Serves 4

675g/1½ lb skinless chicken breast fillets
90ml/6 tbsp tikka paste
60ml/4 tbsp natural (plain) yogurt
30ml/2 tbsp oil
1 onion, chopped
1 garlic clove, crushed
1 fresh green chilli, seeded and chopped

2.5cm/1in piece fresh root ginger, grated
15ml/1 tbsp tomato purée (paste)
15ml/1 tbsp ground almonds
250ml/8fl oz/1 cup water
45ml/3 tbsp butter, melted
50ml/2fl oz/¼ cup double (heavy) cream
15ml/1 tbsp lemon juice
fresh coriander (cilantro) sprigs, natural (plain) yogurt and toasted cumin seeds, to garnish
naan bread, to serve

1 Cut the chicken into 2.5cm/1in cubes. Put 45ml/3 tbsp of the tikka paste and all of the yogurt into a bowl. Add the chicken, turn to coat well and leave to marinate for 20 minutes.

2 For the tikka sauce, heat the oil in a pan and fry the onion, garlic, chilli and ginger for 5 minutes. Add the remaining tikka paste and fry for 2 minutes. Add the tomato purée, ground almonds and water, and simmer for 15 minutes.

3 Meanwhile, thread the chicken on to wooden kebab skewers. Preheat the grill (broiler).

4 Brush the chicken pieces with the butter and grill (broil) under a medium heat for 15 minutes, turning occasionally.

5 Put the tikka sauce into a food processor or blender and process until smooth. Return to the pan and stir in the cream and lemon juice.

6 Remove the chicken pieces from the skewers and add to the sauce, then simmer for 5 minutes. Serve on naan bread and garnish with coriander, yogurt and cumin seeds.

Balti Chilli Chicken

Hot and spicy would be the best way of describing this mouthwatering Balti dish. The smell of the fresh chillies cooking is quite pungent, but delicious.

Serves 4–6

75ml/5 tbsp corn oil
8 large fresh green chillies, slit
2.5ml/½ tsp mixed onion and cumin seeds
4 curry leaves
5ml/1 tsp grated fresh root ginger
5ml/1 tsp chilli powder
5ml/1 tsp ground coriander
5ml/1 tsp crushed garlic
5ml/1 tsp salt
2 medium onions, chopped
675g/1½lb skinless, boneless chicken, cubed
15ml/1 tbsp lemon juice
15ml/1 tbsp roughly chopped fresh mint
15ml/1 tbsp roughly chopped fresh coriander (cilantro)
8–10 cherry tomatoes

1 Heat the oil in a medium karahi or deep, round-based frying pan. Lower the heat slightly and add the slit green chillies. Fry until the skin starts to change colour.

2 Add the onion and cumin seeds, curry leaves, ginger, chilli powder, ground coriander, garlic, salt and onions, and fry for a few seconds, stirring constantly.

3 Add the chicken cubes and stir-fry for 7–10 minutes or until the chicken is cooked right through.

4 Sprinkle the lemon juice over the chicken and add the chopped mint and coriander. Add the cherry tomatoes and serve immediately.

Cook's Tip
A good raita to serve with this can be made by mixing together 1 peeled and diced cucumber, 2 finely diced tomatoes, 1 finely chopped onion, 300ml/½ pint/1¼ cups natural (plain) yogurt, 5ml/1 tsp ground cumin, 5ml/1 tsp lightly fried black mustard seeds and a pinch of salt. Chill before serving.

Chicken Jalfrezi

A Jalfrezi curry is a stir-fried dish cooked with onions, ginger and garlic in a rich pepper sauce.

Serves 4

675g/1½lb skinless chicken
    breast fillets
30ml/2 tbsp oil
5ml/1 tsp cumin seeds
1 onion, finely chopped
1 green (bell) pepper, seeded and
    finely chopped
1 red (bell) pepper, seeded and
    finely chopped
1 garlic clove, crushed
2cm/¾in piece fresh root ginger,
    finely chopped
15ml/1 tbsp curry paste
1.5ml/¼ tsp chilli powder
5ml/1 tsp ground coriander
5ml/1 tsp ground cumin
2.5ml/½ tsp salt
400g/14oz can
    chopped tomatoes
30ml/2 tbsp chopped
    fresh coriander (cilantro)
fresh coriander (cilantro) sprig,
    to garnish
cooked rice, to serve

1 Remove any visible fat from the chicken and cut the meat into 2.5cm/1in cubes.

2 Heat the oil in a wok or frying pan and fry the cumin seeds for 2 minutes until they splutter. Add the onion, peppers, garlic and ginger, and fry for 6–8 minutes.

3 Add the curry paste and fry for about 2 minutes. Stir in the chilli powder, ground coriander, cumin and salt. Add 15ml/1 tbsp water and cook for a further 2 minutes.

4 Add the chicken and cook for about 5 minutes. Add the tomatoes and chopped fresh coriander. Cover and cook for about 15 minutes or until the chicken is tender. Garnish with coriander and serve with rice.

> **Cook's Tip**
> *Curry paste is a "wet" blend of spices cooked with oil and vinegar, which helps to preserve them. Many brands are available from supermarkets and Indian foodstores.*

Chicken Dopiazza

Dopiazza literally translates as "two onions"; in this chicken dish two types of onions are used at different stages during cooking.

Serves 4

45ml/3 tbsp oil
8 small onions, halved
2 bay leaves
8 green cardamom pods
4 cloves
3 dried red chillies
8 black peppercorns
2 onions, finely chopped
2 garlic cloves, crushed
2.5cm/1in piece fresh root ginger,
    finely chopped
5ml/1 tsp ground coriander
5ml/1 tsp ground cumin
2.5ml/½ tsp ground turmeric
2.5ml/½ tsp chilli powder
2.5ml/½ tsp salt
4 tomatoes, peeled and
    finely chopped
120ml/4fl oz/½ cup water
8 skinless chicken pieces, e.g.
    thighs and drumsticks
boiled rice, to serve

1 Heat 30ml/2 tbsp of the oil in a large pan and fry the small onions for 10 minutes or until golden brown. Remove from the pan and set aside.

2 Add the remaining oil to the pan and fry the bay leaves, cardamoms, cloves, chillies and peppercorns for 2 minutes. Add the chopped onions, garlic and ginger and fry for 5 minutes. Stir in the ground spices and salt and cook for 2 minutes.

3 Add the tomatoes and the water and simmer for 5 minutes until the sauce thickens. Add the chicken and cook for about 15 minutes.

4 Add the reserved small onions, then cover and cook for a further 10 minutes or until the chicken is tender. Serve with boiled rice.

Balti Chicken with Lentils

This is rather an unusual combination of flavours, but well worth a try. The sour-tasting mango powder gives a delicious tangy flavour to this spicy dish.

Serves 4–6
75g/3oz/scant ½ cup chana dhal
  (split yellow lentils)
60ml/4 tbsp corn oil
2 medium leeks, chopped
6 large dried red chillies
4 curry leaves
5ml/1 tsp mustard seeds
10ml/2 tsp mango powder
2 medium tomatoes, chopped
2.5ml/½ tsp chilli powder
5ml/1 tsp ground coriander
5ml/1 tsp salt
450g/1lb skinless, boneless
  chicken, cubed
15ml/1 tbsp chopped
  fresh coriander (cilantro)
paratha, to serve

1 Wash the lentils carefully and remove any stones. Put the lentils into a pan with enough water to cover, and boil for about 10 minutes until they are soft but not mushy. Drain and set to one side in a bowl.

2 Heat the oil in a medium karahi or deep, round-based frying pan. Lower the heat slightly and throw in the leeks, dried red chillies, curry leaves and mustard seeds. Stir-fry over a fairly low heat for a few minutes.

3 Add the mango powder, tomatoes, chilli powder, ground coriander, salt and chicken, and stir-fry for 7–10 minutes.

4 Mix in the cooked lentils and fry for a further 2 minutes or until the chicken is cooked right through. Garnish with fresh coriander and serve with paratha.

Cook's Tip
Chana dhal, a split yellow lentil, is available from Asian stores. However, split yellow peas are a good substitute.

Chicken in Spicy Onions

One of the few dishes of India in which onions appear prominently. Chunky onion slices infused with toasted cumin seeds and shredded ginger add a delicious contrast to the flavour of the chicken.

Serves 4–6
1.3kg/3lb chicken, jointed
  and skinned
2.5ml/½ tsp ground turmeric
2.5ml/½ tsp chilli powder
60ml/4 tbsp vegetable oil
4 small onions, finely chopped
175g/6oz/2½ cups coriander
  (cilantro) leaves,
  coarsely chopped
5cm/2in piece fresh root ginger,
  finely shredded
2 fresh green chillies,
  finely chopped
10ml/2 tsp cumin seeds,
  dry roasted
75ml/5 tbsp natural (plain) yogurt
75ml/5 tbsp double
  (heavy) cream
2.5ml/½ tsp cornflour
  (cornstarch)
salt

1 Rub the chicken joints with the turmeric, chilli powder and salt to taste. Heat the oil in a frying pan and fry the chicken pieces, without overlapping, until both sides are sealed. Remove from the pan and keep warm.

2 Reheat the oil and fry 3 of the chopped onions, 150g/5oz/ 2¼ cups of the coriander leaves, half the ginger, the green chillies and the cumin seeds for about 5 minutes until the onions are soft and translucent.

3 Return the chicken to the pan with any juices and mix well. Cover and cook gently for 15 minutes.

4 Remove the pan from the heat and allow to cool a little. Mix together the yogurt, cream and cornflour in a bowl, and gradually fold into the chicken, mixing well.

5 Return the pan to the heat and gently cook until the chicken is tender. Just before serving, stir in the reserved onion, coriander and ginger. Serve hot.

Spicy Masala Chicken

These grilled chicken pieces have a sweet-and-sour taste. They can be served either hot or cold.

Serves 6
12 skinless chicken thighs
90ml/6 tbsp lemon juice
5ml/1 tsp grated fresh root ginger
5ml/1 tsp crushed garlic
5ml/1 tsp crushed dried
   red chillies
5ml/1 tsp salt
5ml/1 tsp soft brown sugar
30ml/2 tbsp clear honey
30ml/2 tbsp chopped
   fresh coriander (cilantro)
1 fresh green chilli,
   finely chopped
30ml/2 tbsp vegetable oil
fresh coriander (cilantro) sprigs,
   to garnish
boiled rice and salad,
   to serve

1 Prick the chicken thighs with a fork. Rinse them in cold water, pat dry with kitchen paper and set aside in a bowl.

2 In a large mixing bowl, thoroughly mix together the lemon juice, grated ginger, garlic, crushed dried red chillies, salt, brown sugar and honey.

3 Transfer the chicken thighs to the spice mixture, turning to coat all over. Set aside in a cool place to marinate for about 45 minutes.

4 Preheat the grill (broiler) to medium. Add the chopped coriander and fresh green chilli to the chicken thighs, and place them in a flameproof dish.

5 Pour any remaining marinade over the chicken and baste with the oil, using a pastry brush.

6 Grill (broil) the chicken thighs for 15–20 minutes, turning and basting with the oil occasionally, until golden brown and the juices run clear when the thickest part is pierced with a skewer or the point of a knife.

7 Transfer to a serving dish, garnish with fresh coriander sprigs and serve with rice and salad.

Hot Chicken Curry

This curry has a lovely, thick sauce and is made using red and green peppers for extra colour. It can be served with either chapatis or plain boiled rice.

Serves 4
30ml/2 tbsp corn oil
1.5ml/¼ tsp fenugreek seeds
1.5ml/¼ tsp onion seeds
2 medium onions, chopped
2.5ml/½ tsp crushed garlic
2.5ml/½ tsp grated fresh
   root ginger
5ml/1 tsp ground coriander
5ml/1 tsp chilli powder
5ml/1 tsp salt
400g/14oz can tomatoes
30ml/2 tbsp lemon juice
350g/12oz skinless, boneless
   chicken, cubed
30ml/2 tbsp chopped
   fresh coriander (cilantro)
3 fresh green chillies, chopped
½ red (bell) pepper, seeded and
   cut into chunks
½ green (bell) pepper, seeded
   and cut into chunks
fresh coriander (cilantro) sprigs,
   to garnish

1 Heat the oil in a heavy pan, and fry the fenugreek and onion seeds until they turn a shade darker. Add the onions, garlic and ginger and fry for about 5 minutes.

2 Meanwhile, in a separate bowl, mix together the ground coriander, chilli powder, salt, tomatoes and lemon juice. Pour the tomato mixture into the pan and stir-fry over a medium heat for about 3 minutes.

3 Add the chicken cubes and stir-fry for 5–7 minutes. Add the chopped fresh coriander, green chopped chillies and peppers. Lower the heat, cover and simmer for about 10 minutes until the chicken is cooked. Serve hot, garnished with coriander sprigs.

> **Cook's Tip**
> *Known as methi in Indian, fenugreek seeds look like small, light brown pebbles and have a pungent smell. It is these seeds that give curry powder its characteristic aroma.*

Balti Chicken in Saffron Sauce

A beautifully aromatic chicken dish that is partly cooked in the oven.

Serves 4–6

50g/2oz/4 tbsp butter
30ml/2 tbsp corn oil
1.3kg/3lb chicken, skinned and
    cut into 8 portions
1 medium onion, chopped
5ml/1 tsp crushed garlic
2.5ml/ ½ tsp crushed
    black peppercorns
2.5ml/ ½ tsp crushed
    cardamom pods

1.5ml/ ¼ tsp ground cinnamon
7.5ml/1½ tsp chilli powder
150ml/ ¼ pint/ ⅔ cup natural
    (plain) yogurt
50g/2oz/ ½ cup ground almonds
15ml/1 tbsp lemon juice
5ml/1 tsp salt
5ml/1 tsp saffron threads
150ml/ ¼ pint/ ⅔ cup water
150ml/ ¼ pint/ ⅔ cup single
    (light) cream
30ml/2 tbsp chopped fresh
    coriander (cilantro)
boiled rice, to serve

1 Preheat the oven to 180°C/350°F/Gas 4. Heat the butter and oil in a medium karahi or deep, round-based frying pan. Add the chicken portions and fry for about 5 minutes until lightly browned. Remove from the pan using a slotted spoon, leaving behind as much of the fat as possible, and set aside.

2 Add the onion to the pan, and fry over a medium heat. Mix together the garlic, peppercorns, cardamom, cinnamon, chilli powder, yogurt, ground almonds, lemon juice, salt and saffron threads in a bowl. When the onions are lightly browned, pour the spice mixture into the pan and stir-fry for about 1 minute. Return the chicken to the pan and continue to stir-fry for a further 2 minutes. Add the water and bring to a simmer.

3 Transfer the contents of the pan to an ovenproof casserole and cover with a lid, or, if using a karahi, cover with foil. Transfer to the oven and cook for 30–35 minutes.

4 When the chicken is cooked through, remove it from the oven. Transfer to a frying pan and stir in the cream. Reheat gently over a low heat for about 2 minutes. Garnish with chopped fresh coriander and serve with boiled rice.

Balti Baby Chicken in Tamarind Sauce

The tamarind in this recipe gives the dish a sweet-and-sour flavour; this is also quite a hot Balti.

Serves 4–6

60ml/4 tbsp tomato ketchup
15ml/1 tbsp tamarind paste
60ml/4 tbsp water
7.5ml/1½ tsp chilli powder
7.5ml/1½ tsp salt
15ml/1 tbsp sugar
7.5ml/1½ tsp grated fresh
    root ginger
7.5ml/1½ tsp crushed garlic
30ml/2 tbsp desiccated
    (dry, unsweetened
    shredded) coconut

30ml/2 tbsp sesame seeds
5ml/1 tsp poppy seeds
5ml/1 tsp ground cumin
7.5ml/1½ tsp ground coriander
2 x 450g/1lb poussins, skinned
    and each cut into 6–8 pieces
75ml/5 tbsp corn oil
25g/1oz/8 tbsp curry leaves
2.5ml/ ½ tsp onion seeds
3 large dried red chillies
2.5ml/ ½ tsp fenugreek seeds
10–12 cherry tomatoes
45ml/3 tbsp chopped
    fresh coriander (cilantro)
2 fresh green chillies, chopped

1 Put the tomato ketchup, tamarind paste and water into a large bowl and blend well. Stir in the chilli powder, salt, sugar, ginger, garlic, coconut, sesame seeds, poppy seeds, ground cumin and ground coriander. Add the poussins and stir until they are well coated with the spice mixture. Set aside.

2 Heat the oil in a large karahi or deep, round-based frying pan. Add the curry leaves, onion seeds, dried red chillies and fenugreek seeds and fry for about 1 minute.

3 Lower the heat to medium and add the poussins, 2–3 pieces at a time, with their sauce, mixing as you go. When all the pieces are in the pan, stir well with a slotted spoon.

4 Simmer gently for about 12–15 minutes or until the poussins are thoroughly cooked. Finally, add the tomatoes, fresh coriander and green chillies, and serve.

Spicy Chicken Dhal

The chicken is coated in a spiced lentil sauce and finished with a tarka, a seasoned oil, which is poured over the dish just before serving.

Serves 4
30ml/2 tbsp chana dhal (split yellow lentils)
50g/2oz/¼ cup masoor dhal
15ml/1 tbsp corn oil
2 medium onions, chopped
5ml/1 tsp crushed garlic
5ml/1 tsp grated fresh root ginger
2.5ml/½ tsp ground turmeric
7.5ml/1½ tsp chilli powder
5ml/1 tsp garam masala
2.5ml/½ tsp ground coriander
7.5ml/1½ tsp salt
175g/6oz skinless chicken breast fillets, cubed
45ml/3 tbsp fresh coriander (cilantro) leaves
1–2 fresh green chillies, seeded and chopped
30–45ml/2–3 tbsp lemon juice
300ml/½ pint/1¼ cups water
2 tomatoes, peeled and halved

For the tarka
5ml/1 tsp corn oil
2.5ml/½ tsp cumin seeds
2 garlic cloves
2 dried red chillies
4 curry leaves

1 Boil the chana dhal and masoor dhal together in a pan of water until soft and mushy. Set aside.

2 Heat the oil in a wok or frying pan and fry the onions until soft and golden brown. Stir in the garlic, ginger, turmeric, chilli powder, garam masala, ground coriander and salt. Add the chicken cubes and stir-fry for 5–7 minutes.

3 Add half the fresh coriander, the green chillies, lemon juice and water and cook for a further 3–5 minutes.

4 Pour in the chana dhal and masoor dhal, followed by the tomatoes. Add the remaining fresh coriander. Remove from the heat and set aside.

5 To make the tarka, heat the oil and add the cumin seeds, whole garlic cloves, dried chillies and curry leaves. Heat for about 30 seconds and, while it is still hot, pour it over the top of the chicken and lentils. Serve immediately.

Balti Chicken Vindaloo

This is considered rather a hot curry and is probably one of the best-known Indian dishes, especially in the West.

Serves 4
1 large potato
150ml/¼ pint/⅔ cup malt vinegar
7.5ml/1½ tsp crushed coriander seeds
5ml/1 tsp crushed cumin seeds
7.5ml/1½ tsp chilli powder
1.5ml/¼ tsp ground turmeric
5ml/1 tsp crushed garlic
5ml/1 tsp grated fresh root ginger
5ml/1 tsp salt
7.5ml/1½ tsp paprika
15ml/1 tbsp tomato purée (paste)
large pinch of ground fenugreek
300ml/½ pint/1¼ cups water
225g/8oz skinless chicken breast fillets, cubed
15ml/1 tbsp corn oil
2 medium onions, sliced
4 curry leaves
2 fresh green chillies, chopped

1 Peel the potato, cut it into large, irregular shapes, place in a bowl of water and set aside.

2 In a bowl, mix the vinegar with the coriander and cumin seeds, chilli powder, turmeric, garlic, ginger, salt, paprika, tomato purée, fenugreek and water. Pour this mixture over the chicken and set aside.

3 Heat the oil in a wok or frying pan and fry the onions with the curry leaves for 3–4 minutes.

4 Lower the heat and add the chicken mixture to the pan. Continue to stir for a further 2 minutes. Drain the potato pieces and add to the pan. Cover and cook over a medium to low heat for 5–7 minutes or until the sauce has thickened slightly, and the chicken and potatoes are cooked through. Stir the chopped green chillies into the dish and serve hot.

Cook's Tip
The best thing to drink with a hot curry is either iced water or a yogurt-based lassi.

Balti Minced Chicken with Green & Red Chillies

Minced chicken is seldom cooked in Indian or Pakistani homes. However, it works very well in this low-fat recipe.

Serves 4
275g/10oz skinless chicken
 breast fillet, cubed
2 thick fresh red chillies
3 thick fresh green chillies
30ml/2 tbsp corn oil
6 curry leaves
3 medium onions, sliced
7.5ml/1½ tsp crushed garlic
7.5ml/1½ tsp ground coriander
7.5ml/1½ tsp grated fresh
 root ginger
5ml/1 tsp chilli powder
5ml/1 tsp salt
15ml/1 tbsp lemon juice
30ml/2 tbsp chopped
 fresh coriander (cilantro)
chapatis and lemon wedges,
 to serve

1 Place the chicken cubes in a pan, cover with water and bring to the boil. Lower the heat and simmer for about 10 minutes until tender and cooked through. Drain thoroughly. Place the chicken in a food processor and mince (grind).

2 Cut the chillies in half lengthways and, if desired, remove the seeds. Cut the flesh into strips.

3 Heat the oil in a non-stick wok or frying pan and fry the curry leaves and onions until the onions are a soft golden brown. Lower the heat and add the garlic, ground coriander, ginger, chilli powder and salt.

4 Add the minced (ground) chicken and stir-fry over a low heat for 3–5 minutes. Add the lemon juice, chilli strips and most of the fresh coriander. Stir for a further 3–5 minutes.

5 Transfer to a warmed serving dish and serve immediately, garnished with the remaining fresh coriander and accompanied by chapatis and lemon wedges.

Balti Chicken Pieces with Cumin & Coriander Potatoes

The spicy potatoes are cooked separately in the oven first.

Serves 4
150ml/¼ pint/⅔ cup natural
 (plain) low-fat yogurt
25g/1oz/¼ cup ground almonds
7.5ml/1½ tsp ground coriander
2.5ml/½ tsp chilli powder
5ml/1 tsp garam masala
15ml/1 tbsp coconut milk
5ml/1 tsp crushed garlic
5ml/1 tsp grated fresh root ginger
30ml/2 tbsp chopped fresh
 coriander (cilantro)
1 fresh red chilli, seeded
 and chopped
225g/8oz skinless chicken
 breast fillets, cubed
15ml/1 tbsp corn oil
2 medium onions, sliced
3 green cardamom pods
2.5cm/1in cinnamon stick
2 cloves

For the potatoes
15ml/1 tbsp corn oil
8 baby potatoes, thickly sliced
1.5ml/¼ tsp cumin seeds
15ml/1 tbsp finely chopped
 fresh coriander (cilantro)

1 In a bowl, mix together the yogurt, ground almonds, ground coriander, chilli powder, garam masala, coconut milk, garlic, ginger, half the fresh coriander and half the chilli. Add the chicken cubes, mix well and leave to marinate for 2 hours.

2 Meanwhile, for the potatoes, preheat the oven to 180°C/350°F/Gas 4. Heat the oil in a non-stick wok or frying pan and stir-fry the potatoes, cumin seeds and coriander for 2–3 minutes. Transfer to an ovenproof dish, cover and cook in the oven for about 30 minutes or until cooked through.

3 Increase the oven temperature to 200°C/400°F/Gas 6. Wipe out the wok or frying pan and add the oil with the onions, cardamoms, cinnamon and cloves. Heat for about 1½ minutes. Pour the chicken mixture into the onions and stir-fry for 5–7 minutes. Lower the heat, cover and cook gently for a further 5–7 minutes. Serve, topped with the cooked potatoes, and garnished with the remaining chopped fresh coriander and red chilli.

Balti Chicken Pasanda

Pasanda dishes are firm favourites in Pakistan, but they are also becoming well known in the West.

Serves 4

60ml/4 tbsp Greek (US strained plain) yogurt
2.5ml/ ½ tsp black cumin seeds
4 cardamom pods
6 black peppercorns
10ml/2 tsp garam masala
2.5cm/1in cinnamon stick
15ml/1 tbsp ground almonds
5ml/1 tsp crushed garlic
5ml/1 tsp grated fresh root ginger
5ml/1 tsp chilli powder
5ml/1 tsp salt
675g/1½lb skinless, boneless chicken, cubed
75ml/5 tbsp corn oil
2 medium onions, diced
3 fresh green chillies, chopped
30ml/2 tbsp chopped fresh coriander (cilantro), plus extra to garnish
120ml/4fl oz/ ½ cup single (light) cream

1 Mix the yogurt, cumin seeds, cardamoms, peppercorns, garam masala, cinnamon stick, ground almonds, garlic, ginger, chilli powder and salt in a medium bowl. Add the chicken, stirring to coat and set aside to marinate for about 2 hours.

2 Heat the oil in a large karahi or deep, round-based frying pan. Add the onions and fry over a medium heat for 2–3 minutes until just softened.

3 Pour in the chicken mixture and stir until it is well blended with the onions. Cook over a medium heat for 12–15 minutes or until the sauce thickens and the chicken is cooked through.

4 Add the green chillies and fresh coriander, and pour in the cream. Bring to the boil and serve immediately, garnished with more coriander.

> **Cook's Tip**
> *Ground ginger is no substitute for the fresh root, as it burns very easily. Wrap fresh root ginger, unpeeled, in clear film (plastic wrap) and store in the refrigerator for up to 6 weeks.*

Chicken in a Hot Red Sauce

In India, small chickens are used for this dish and served as an individual appetizer with chapatis. If you wish to serve it as a first course, use four poussins instead of chicken joints. Skin them first and make small gashes with a sharp knife to enable the spices to seep in.

Serves 4–6

20ml/4 tsp Kashmiri masala paste
60ml/4 tbsp tomato ketchup
5ml/1 tsp Worcestershire sauce
5ml/1 tsp Indian five-spice powder
5ml/1 tsp sugar
8 skinless chicken portions
45ml/3 tbsp vegetable oil
4 garlic cloves, crushed
5cm/2in piece fresh root ginger, finely shredded
juice of 1 lemon
a few fresh coriander (cilantro) leaves, finely chopped
salt

1 In a bowl, mix together the Kashmiri masala, tomato ketchup, Worcestershire sauce, five-spice powder, sugar and salt. Set aside in a warm place until the sugar has dissolved.

2 Place the chicken portions in a wide, shallow dish and rub with the spice mixture. Set aside to marinate for 2 hours or overnight if possible.

3 Heat the oil in a large frying pan and fry the garlic and half the ginger until golden brown. Add the chicken pieces and the marinade and fry, without overlapping, until both sides are sealed. Cover the pan and cook gently until the chicken is nearly tender and the gravy clings, with the oil separating.

4 Sprinkle the chicken with the lemon juice, the remaining ginger and coriander leaves. Mix well, reheat and serve hot.

Hot Chilli Chicken

Not for the faint-hearted, this fiery, hot curry is made with a rich and spicy chilli masala paste.

Serves 4
30ml/2 tbsp tomato
  purée (paste)
2 garlic cloves, roughly chopped
2 fresh green chillies,
  roughly chopped
5 dried red chillies
2.5ml/ ½ tsp salt
1.5ml/ ¼ tsp sugar
5ml/1 tsp chilli powder
2.5ml/ ½ tsp paprika
15ml/1 tbsp curry paste

30ml/2 tbsp oil
2.5ml/ ½ tsp cumin seeds
1 onion, finely chopped
2 bay leaves
5ml/1 tsp ground coriander
5ml/1 tsp ground cumin
1.5ml/ ¼ tsp ground turmeric
400g/14oz can
  chopped tomatoes
150ml/ ¼ pint/ ⅔ cup water
8 skinless chicken thighs
5ml/1 tsp garam masala
sliced fresh green chillies,
  to garnish
chapatis and natural (plain)
  yogurt, to serve

1 Put the tomato purée, garlic, fresh and dried chillies, salt, sugar, chilli powder, paprika and curry paste into a food processor or blender and process to a smooth paste.

2 Heat the oil in a large pan and fry the cumin seeds for 2 minutes. Add the onion and bay leaves, and fry over a medium heat for about 5 minutes.

3 Add the spice paste and fry for 2–3 minutes. Add the remaining ground spices and cook for 2 minutes. Add the chopped tomatoes and water. Bring to the boil and simmer for 5 minutes until the sauce thickens.

4 Add the chicken and garam masala. Cover and simmer for 25–30 minutes until the chicken is tender. Serve with chapatis and natural yogurt, garnished with sliced green chillies.

Chicken with Ginger & Lemon Grass

This Vietnamese dish can also be prepared using duck legs. Be sure to remove the jointed parts of the drumsticks and thigh bones to make the meat easier to eat with chopsticks.

Serves 4–6
3 chicken legs (thighs
  and drumsticks)
15ml/1 tbsp vegetable oil
2cm/ ¾in piece fresh root ginger,
  finely chopped
1 garlic clove, crushed
1 small fresh red chilli, seeded
  and finely chopped

5cm/2in piece lemon
  grass, shredded
150ml/ ¼ pint/ ⅔ cup
  chicken stock
15ml/1 tbsp fish sauce (optional)
10ml/2 tsp sugar
2.5ml/ ½ tsp salt
juice of ½ lemon
50g/2oz/ ½ cup raw peanuts
2 spring onions
  (scallions), shredded
thinly pared rind of 1 mandarin
  orange or satsuma, shredded
30ml/2 tbsp chopped fresh mint
cooked rice or rice noodles,
  to serve

1 Using the heel of a knife, chop through the narrow end of the chicken drumsticks. Remove the jointed parts of the drumsticks and thigh bones, then remove the skin.

2 Heat the vegetable oil in a large wok or frying pan. Add the chicken, ginger, garlic, chilli and lemon grass, and cook over a medium heat for 3–4 minutes. Add the chicken stock, fish sauce, if using, sugar, salt and lemon juice. Cover and simmer for 30–35 minutes.

3 Grill (broil) or roast the peanuts under a steady heat for about 2–3 minutes until evenly browned. Turn the nuts out on to a clean dishtowel and, when cool enough to handle, rub briskly to loosen the skins. Discard the skins.

4 Serve the chicken, sprinkled with the peanuts, spring onions, the shredded rind of the mandarin orange or satsuma and mint. Serve with rice or rice noodles.

Fragrant Chicken Curry with Thai Spices

To create this wonderful, aromatic dish you need Thai red curry paste – home-made is best, but for speed you could use ready-made.

Serves 4

45ml/3 tbsp oil
I onion, roughly chopped
2 garlic cloves, crushed
I5ml/I tbsp ready-made Thai red curry paste
II5g/4oz creamed coconut (coconut cream) dissolved in about 900ml/I½ pints/3¾ cups boiling water
2 lemon grass stalks, roughly chopped
6 kaffir lime leaves, chopped
I50ml/ ¼ pint/ ⅔ cup Greek (US strained plain) yogurt
30ml/2 tbsp apricot jam
I cooked chicken, about I.5kg/3½lb
30ml/2 tbsp chopped fresh coriander (cilantro)
salt and freshly ground black pepper
kaffir lime leaves, shredded coconut and fresh coriander (cilantro), to garnish
boiled rice, to serve

I Heat the oil in a pan. Add the onion and garlic, and fry over a low heat for 5–10 minutes until soft. Stir in the curry paste and cook, stirring, for 2–3 minutes. Stir in the diluted creamed coconut, then add the lemon grass, lime leaves, yogurt and apricot jam. Stir well. Cover and simmer for 30 minutes.

2 Process the sauce in a blender or food processor, then strain it back into a clean pan, pressing as much of the puréed mixture as possible through the sieve.

3 Remove the skin from the chicken. Slice the meat off the bones and cut it into bitesize pieces. Add to the sauce. If the sauce seems too thin, add a little more creamed coconut.

4 Bring the sauce back to simmering point. Stir in the fresh coriander, and season to taste with salt and pepper. Serve with boiled rice, garnished with extra lime leaves, shredded coconut and fresh coriander.

Thai Chicken & Vegetable Curry

For this curry, chicken and vegetables are cooked in an aromatic Thai-spiced coconut sauce.

Serves 4

I5ml/I tbsp sunflower oil
6 shallots, finely chopped
2 garlic cloves, crushed
450g/Ilb chicken breast fillets, cut into Icm/½in cubes
5ml/I tsp ground coriander
5ml/I tsp ground cumin
20ml/4 tsp ready-made Thai green curry paste
I green (bell) pepper, seeded and diced
I75g/6oz baby sweetcorn, halved
II5g/4oz green beans, halved
I50ml/ ¼ pint/ ⅔ cup chicken stock
I50ml/ ¼ pint/ ⅔ cup coconut milk
30ml/2 tbsp cornflour (cornstarch)
fresh herb sprigs and toasted cashew nuts, to garnish
boiled rice, to serve

I Heat the oil in a pan, add the shallots, garlic and chicken, and cook for 5 minutes until the chicken is coloured all over, stirring occasionally. Add the coriander, cumin and curry paste, and cook for I minute.

2 Add the green pepper, baby sweetcorn, beans, stock and coconut milk, and stir to mix. Bring to the boil, stirring constantly, then cover and simmer for 20–30 minutes until the chicken is tender, stirring occasionally.

3 Blend the cornflour with about 45ml/3 tbsp water in a small bowl. Stir into the curry, then simmer gently for about 2 minutes, stirring constantly, until the sauce thickens slightly. Serve hot, garnished with fresh herb sprigs and toasted cashew nuts, and accompanied by boiled rice.

Chicken Cooked in Coconut Milk

Traditionally, the chicken for this dish would be part-cooked by frying, but here it is roasted in the oven. This is an unusual recipe in that the sauce is white, as it does not contain chillies or turmeric, unlike many other Indonesian dishes.

Serves 4
1.5kg/3½lb chicken or
   4 chicken quarters
4 garlic cloves
1 onion, sliced
4 macadamia nuts or 8 almonds
15ml/1 tbsp coriander seeds,
   dry-fried, or 5ml/1 tsp
   ground coriander
45ml/3 tbsp oil
2.5cm/1in piece fresh galangal,
   peeled and bruised
2 lemon grass stalks, fleshy
   part bruised
3 kaffir lime leaves
2 bay leaves
5ml/1 tsp sugar
600ml/1 pint/2½ cups
   coconut milk
salt
boiled rice and deep-fried onions,
   to serve

1 Preheat the oven to 190°C/375°F/Gas 5. If using a whole chicken, cut it into 4 or 8 pieces. Season with salt. Put it into an oiled roasting pan and roast for 25–30 minutes.

2 Meanwhile, prepare the sauce. Grind the garlic, onion, nuts and coriander to a fine paste in a food processor or using a pestle and mortar. Heat the oil in a frying pan and fry the paste to bring out the flavour. Do not allow it to brown.

3 Add the part-cooked chicken pieces to a wok, together with the galangal, lemon grass, lime and bay leaves, sugar, coconut milk and salt to taste. Mix well to coat in the sauce.

4 Bring to the boil, then reduce the heat and simmer gently for 30–40 minutes, uncovered, until the chicken is tender and the coconut sauce is reduced and thickened. Stir the mixture occasionally during cooking.

5 Just before serving, remove and discard the galangal and lemon grass. Serve with boiled rice and sprinkle with crisp deep-fried onions.

Green Curry Coconut Chicken

The recipe given here for green curry paste is a slightly complex one, so allow time to make it properly – your efforts will be well rewarded.

Serves 4–6
1.2kg/2½lb chicken
600ml/1 pint/2½ cups canned
   coconut milk
450ml/¾ pint/scant 2 cups
   chicken stock
2 kaffir lime leaves
350g/12oz sweet potatoes,
   peeled and roughly chopped
350g/12oz winter squash, peeled,
   seeded and roughly chopped
115g/4oz green beans, halved
1 small bunch fresh coriander
   (cilantro), shredded, to garnish

For the green curry paste
10ml/2 tsp coriander seeds
2.5ml/½ tsp caraway or
   cumin seeds
3–4 medium fresh green chillies,
   finely chopped
20ml/4 tsp sugar
10ml/2 tsp salt
7.5cm/3in piece lemon grass
2cm/¾in piece galangal or fresh
   ginger, finely chopped
3 garlic cloves, crushed
4 shallots or 1 medium onion,
   finely chopped
2cm/¾in shrimp paste cube
45ml/3 tbsp finely chopped
   fresh coriander (cilantro)
45ml/3 tbsp finely chopped fresh
   fresh mint or basil
2.5ml/½ tsp grated nutmeg
30ml/2 tbsp vegetable oil

1 To prepare the chicken, remove the legs, then separate the thighs from the drumsticks. Separate the lower part of the chicken carcass by cutting through the rib section with kitchen scissors. Divide the breast part in half down the middle, then chop each half in two. Remove the skin from all the pieces. Set the chicken aside.

2 Strain the coconut milk into a bowl, reserving the thick part. Place the chicken in a stainless steel or enamel pan, cover with the thin part of the coconut milk and the stock. Add the lime leaves and simmer, uncovered, for 40 minutes. Lift the chicken out of the pan, cut the meat off the bones and set aside. Reserve the stock.

3 To make the green curry paste, dry-fry the coriander and caraway or cumin seeds. Grind the chillies with the sugar and salt in a food processor or using a pestle and mortar to make a smooth paste. Combine the dry-fried seeds with the chillies, add the lemon grass, galangal or ginger, garlic and shallots or onion, then grind smoothly. Add the shrimp paste, chopped herbs, nutmeg and oil.

4 Place 250ml/8fl oz/1 cup of the reserved chicken stock in a large wok. Add 60–75ml/4–5 tbsp of the curry paste to the liquid according to taste. Boil rapidly until the liquid has reduced completely. Add the remaining chicken stock, the chicken meat, sweet potatoes, squash and beans. Simmer for 10–15 minutes until all the vegetables are cooked.

5 Just before serving, stir in the thick part of the coconut milk and simmer gently to thicken. Serve, garnished with the shredded coriander.

Red Chicken Curry with Bamboo Shoots

Bamboo shoots have a lovely, crunchy texture. It is quite acceptable to use canned ones, as fresh bamboo is not readily available in the West. Buy canned whole bamboo shoots, which are crisper and of better quality than sliced shoots. Rinse well before using.

Serves 4–6

1 litre/1¾ pints/4 cups coconut milk
450g/1lb skinless chicken breast fillets, cut into bitesize pieces
30ml/2 tbsp Thai fish sauce (nam pla)
15ml/1 tbsp sugar
225g/8oz drained canned bamboo shoots, rinsed and sliced
5 kaffir lime leaves, torn
salt and freshly ground black pepper
chopped fresh red chillies and kaffir lime leaves, to garnish

For the red curry paste
5ml/1 tsp coriander seeds
2.5ml/½ tsp cumin seeds
12–15 fresh red chillies, seeded and roughly chopped
4 shallots, thinly sliced
2 garlic cloves, chopped
15ml/1 tbsp chopped galangal
2 lemon grass stalks, chopped
3 kaffir lime leaves, chopped
4 fresh coriander (cilantro) roots
10 black peppercorns
good pinch of ground cinnamon
5ml/1 tsp ground turmeric
2.5ml/½ tsp shrimp paste
5ml/1 tsp salt
30ml/2 tbsp vegetable oil

1 To make the red curry paste, dry-fry the coriander and cumin seeds for 1–2 minutes, then put in a mortar or food processor with all the remaining ingredients, except the oil. Pound or process to a paste.

2 Add the oil, a little at a time, mixing or processing well after each addition. Transfer to a jar and place in the refrigerator until ready to use.

3 Pour half of the coconut milk into a large pan. Bring to the boil, stirring constantly until the milk has separated.

4 Stir in 30ml/2 tbsp of the red curry paste and cook the mixture for 2–3 minutes, stirring constantly. (The remaining red curry paste can be stored in the refrigerator for 3–4 weeks.)

5 Add the chicken pieces, fish sauce and sugar to the pan. Mix well, then cook for 5–6 minutes until the chicken changes colour and is cooked through, stirring constantly to prevent the mixture from sticking to the base of the pan.

6 Pour the remaining coconut milk into the pan, then add the bamboo shoots and kaffir lime leaves. Bring back to the boil over a medium heat, stirring constantly to prevent the mixture from sticking, then taste and add salt and pepper if necessary.

7 To serve, spoon the curry into a warmed serving dish and garnish with chopped chillies and kaffir lime leaves.

Chicken with Spices & Soy Sauce

A very simple Indonesian recipe, which often appears on Padang restaurant menus. Any leftovers taste equally good when reheated the following day.

Serves 4

1.5kg/3½lb chicken, jointed and cut into 16 pieces
3 onions, sliced
about 1 litre/1¾ pints/ 4 cups water
3 garlic cloves, crushed
3–4 fresh red chillies, seeded and sliced, or 15ml/1 tbsp chilli powder
45–60ml/3–4 tbsp oil
2.5ml/½ tsp grated nutmeg
6 cloves
5ml/1 tsp tamarind pulp, soaked in 45ml/3 tbsp warm water
30–45ml/2–3 tbsp dark or light soy sauce
salt
fresh red chilli shreds, to garnish
boiled rice, to serve

1 Place the chicken pieces in a large pan with one of the onions. Pour over enough water just to cover. Bring to the boil, then reduce the heat and simmer gently for 20 minutes.

2 Process the remaining onions, with the garlic and chillies, to a fine paste in a food processor or using a pestle and mortar. Heat a little of the oil in a wok or frying pan and cook the paste to bring out the flavour, but do not allow it to brown.

3 When the chicken has cooked for 20 minutes, lift it out of the stock in the pan, using a slotted spoon, and put it straight into the spicy mixture. Toss everything together over a fairly high heat so that the spices permeate the chicken pieces. Reserve 300ml/½ pint/1¼ cups of the chicken stock.

4 Stir the nutmeg and cloves into the chicken. Strain the tamarind, and add the tamarind juice and the soy sauce to the chicken. Cook for a further 2–3 minutes, then add the reserved stock.

5 Taste and adjust the seasoning and cook, uncovered, for a further 25–35 minutes until the chicken pieces are tender. Transfer the chicken to a serving bowl, top with shredded chilli and serve with boiled rice.

CHICKEN WITH RICE, PASTA & NOODLES

Spicy dishes of chicken with rice or noodles are not surprising – you have only to think of Chicken Biriyani and Chicken Chow Mein – but pasta dishes are a little more unusual. However, like rice and noodles, the blandness of pasta lends itself to the assertive flavourings of all kinds of spices, from ginger to cayenne and from chillies to saffron. The emphasis in this chapter is, therefore, not so much on the fiery as on the flavoursome, although not all the heat has gone out of the kitchen. In fact, all the recipes in this chapter provide a wonderful opportunity for the adventurous cook to make variety the spice of life, and many also have the advantage of being a meal in themselves. Why not serve spectacular Indonesian Pineapple Rice next time friends visit, or surprise the family with a Japanese Chicken & Mushroom Donburi? Familiar favourites and classic dishes have their place, too – a tongue-tingling jambalaya, a fragrant korma, peppery Sichuan noodles and hot Caribbean chicken, for example. There are substantial dishes for a family supper, quick and easy recipes for midweek meals and special-occasion dishes – every one of them seasoned to taste.

Thai Fried Rice

This recipe uses Thai fragrant rice, which is sometimes known as jasmine rice.

Serves 4
50g/2oz/ ½ cup coconut
   milk powder
475ml/16fl oz/2 cups water
350g/12oz/1⅔ cups Thai
   fragrant rice
30ml/2 tbsp groundnut
   (peanut) oil
2 garlic cloves, chopped
115g/4oz/⅔ cup baby sweetcorn
   cobs, sliced

1 small onion, finely chopped
2.5cm/1in piece fresh root
   ginger, grated
225g/8oz skinless chicken breast
   fillets, cut into 1cm/½in dice
1 red (bell) pepper, seeded
   and diced
115g/4oz/⅔ cup drained canned
   sweetcorn kernels
5ml/1 tsp chilli oil
15ml/1 tbsp hot curry powder
salt
2 eggs, beaten
spring onion (scallion) shreds,
   to garnish

1 In a pan, whisk the coconut milk powder into the water. Add the rice, bring to the boil and stir once. Lower the heat to a gentle simmer, cover and cook for 10 minutes or until the rice is tender and the liquid has been absorbed. Spread the rice on a baking sheet and leave until completely cold.

2 Heat the oil in a wok, add the garlic, sweetcorn cobs, onion and ginger, and stir-fry for 2 minutes. Push the vegetables to the sides of the wok, add the chicken to the centre and stir-fry for 2 minutes. Add the rice and stir-fry over a high heat for 3 minutes.

3 Stir in the red pepper, sweetcorn kernels, chilli oil and curry powder, and season with salt. Toss over the heat for another 1 minute. Stir in the beaten egg and cook for 1 minute more. Garnish with spring onion shreds and serve.

> **Cook's Tip**
> *The rice must be completely cold before it is fried and the oil should be very hot, or the rice will absorb too much oil.*

Chicken & Basil Coconut Rice

For this dish the rice is partially boiled before being simmered with coconut to blend the flavours. Serve in a halved coconut.

Serves 4
350g/12oz/1⅔ cups Thai
   fragrant rice
30–45ml/2–3 tbsp groundnut oil
1 large onion, thinly sliced
   into rings
1 garlic clove, crushed
1 fresh red chilli, seeded and
   thinly sliced

1 fresh green chilli, seeded and
   thinly sliced
generous handful of basil leaves
about 350g/12oz skinned chicken
   breast fillets, thinly sliced
5mm/¼in piece lemon grass,
   pounded or finely chopped
50g/2oz block creamed coconut
   (coconut cream) dissolved in
   600ml/1 pint/2½ cups
   boiling water
salt and freshly ground
   black pepper

1 Bring a pan of water to the boil. Add the rice to the pan and boil for about 6 minutes until partially cooked. Drain and allow to cool.

2 Heat the oil in a frying pan and fry the onion rings for 5–10 minutes until golden and crisp. Lift out using a slotted spoon, drain on kitchen paper and set aside, but keep warm.

3 Fry the garlic and chillies in the oil remaining in the pan for 2–3 minutes, then add the basil leaves and fry briefly until they begin to wilt. Remove a few leaves and set them aside for the garnish, then add the chicken slices and lemon grass to the pan and fry for 2–3 minutes until golden.

4 Add the rice. Stir-fry for a few minutes to coat the grains, then pour in the coconut liquid. Cook for 4–5 minutes or until the rice is tender, adding a little more water if necessary.

5 Adjust the seasoning to taste. Pile the rice into a halved coconut or warmed serving dish, sprinkle with the fried onion rings and reserved basil leaves, and serve immediately.

Indonesian Pineapple Rice

This way of presenting rice not only looks spectacular, it also tastes so delicious that it can easily be served solo.

Serves 4
75g/3oz/¾ cup unsalted peanuts
1 large pineapple
45ml/3 tbsp groundnut (peanut) or sunflower oil
1 onion, chopped
1 garlic clove, crushed

about 225g/8oz chicken breast fillets, cut into strips
225g/8oz/generous 1 cup Thai fragrant rice
600ml/1 pint/2½ cups chicken stock
1 lemon grass stalk, bruised
2 thick slices ham, cut into julienne strips
1 fresh red chilli, seeded and very thinly sliced
salt

1 Dry-fry the peanuts in a non-stick frying pan until golden. When cool, grind one-sixth of them in a coffee or spice mill and chop the remainder.

2 Cut a lengthways slice of pineapple, slicing through the leaves, then cut out the flesh to leave a neat shell. Chop 115g/4oz of the pineapple into cubes, saving the remainder for another dish.

3 Heat the oil in a pan and fry the onion and garlic for 3–4 minutes until soft. Add the chicken strips and stir-fry over a medium heat for a few minutes until evenly brown.

4 Add the rice to the pan. Toss with the chicken mixture for a few minutes, then pour in the stock and add the lemon grass and a little salt. Bring to just below boiling point, lower the heat, cover the pan and simmer gently for 10–12 minutes until both the rice and the chicken pieces are tender.

5 Stir the chopped peanuts, the pineapple cubes and the ham into the rice, then spoon the mixture into the pineapple shell. Sprinkle the ground peanuts and the sliced chilli over the top, and serve immediately.

Chicken Biryani

A classic rice and chicken dish, prepared with whole and ground spices and finished in the oven.

Serves 4
275g/10oz/1½ cups basmati rice
2.5ml/½ tsp salt
5 whole cardamom pods
2–3 whole cloves
1 cinnamon stick
45ml/3 tbsp vegetable oil
3 onions, sliced
675g/1½lb skinned chicken breast fillets, cubed
1.5ml/¼ tsp ground cloves
5 cardamom pods, seeds removed and ground
1.5ml/¼ tsp hot chilli powder
5ml/1 tsp ground cumin

5ml/1 tsp ground coriander
2.5ml/½ tsp freshly ground black pepper
3 garlic cloves, finely chopped
5ml/1 tsp finely chopped fresh root ginger
juice of 1 lemon
4 tomatoes, sliced
30ml/2 tbsp chopped fresh coriander (cilantro)
150ml/¼ pint/⅔ cup natural (plain) yogurt
2.5ml/½ tsp saffron threads, soaked in 10ml/2 tsp hot milk
150ml/¼ pint/⅔ cup water
45ml/3 tbsp toasted flaked (sliced) almonds and fresh coriander (cilantro) sprigs, to garnish
natural (plain) yogurt, to serve

1 Preheat the oven to 190°C/375°F/Gas 5. Bring a pan of water to the boil and add the rice, salt, whole cardamom pods, whole cloves and cinnamon stick. Boil for 2 minutes and then drain, leaving the whole spices in the rice.

2 Heat the oil in a large frying pan and fry the onions for 8 minutes until browned. Add the chicken, then all the ground spices, the garlic, ginger and lemon juice. Stir-fry for 5 minutes.

3 Transfer the mixture to a casserole. Lay the tomatoes on top, sprinkle with the coriander, spoon over the yogurt and top with the drained rice. Drizzle the saffron and milk over the rice and pour over the water. Cover and bake for 1 hour.

4 Transfer the rice to a warmed serving platter and discard the whole spices. Garnish with toasted almonds and fresh coriander and serve with yogurt.

Chicken & Mushroom Donburi

"Donburi" means a one-dish meal that is eaten from a bowl, and takes its name from the eponymous Japanese porcelain food bowl. As in most Japanese dishes, the rice here is completely plain, but is nevertheless an integral part of the dish.

Serves 4

225–275g/8–10oz/generous 1–1½ cups Japanese rice or Thai fragrant rice
10ml/2 tsp groundnut (peanut) oil
50g/2oz/4 tbsp butter
2 garlic cloves, crushed
2.5cm/1in piece fresh root ginger, grated
5 spring onions (scallions), sliced diagonally
1 fresh green chilli, seeded and thinly sliced
3 skinless chicken breast fillets, cut into thin strips
150g/5oz tofu, cut into small cubes
115g/4oz/1¾ cups shiitake mushrooms, stalks discarded and cups sliced
15ml/1 tbsp Japanese rice wine
30ml/2 tbsp light soy sauce
10ml/2 tsp granulated sugar
400ml/14fl oz/1⅔ cups chicken stock

1 Cook the rice following the instructions on the packet.

2 Meanwhile, heat the oil and butter in a large frying pan. Stir-fry the garlic, ginger, spring onions and chilli for 1–2 minutes until slightly softened. Add the chicken and fry, in batches if necessary, until all the pieces are evenly browned.

3 Using a slotted spoon, transfer the chicken mixture to a plate and add the tofu to the pan. Stir-fry for a few minutes, then add the mushrooms. Stir-fry for 2–3 minutes over a medium heat until the mushrooms are tender.

4 Stir in the rice wine, soy sauce and sugar, and cook briskly for 1–2 minutes, stirring. Return the chicken to the pan, toss over the heat for about 2 minutes, then pour in the stock. Stir well and cook over a gentle heat for 5–6 minutes until bubbling.

5 Spoon the rice into individual serving bowls and pile the chicken mixture and sauce on top.

Caribbean Chicken with Pigeon Pea Rice

Golden, spicy caramelized chicken tops a richly flavoured vegetable rice in this hearty and delicious supper dish.

Serves 4

5ml/1 tsp ground allspice
2.5ml/½ tsp ground cinnamon
5ml/1 tsp dried thyme
pinch of ground cloves
1.5ml/¼ tsp freshly grated nutmeg
4 skinless chicken breast fillets
45ml/3 tbsp groundnut (peanut) or sunflower oil
15g/½oz/1 tbsp butter
1 onion, chopped
2 garlic cloves, crushed
1 carrot, diced
1 celery stick, chopped
3 spring onions (scallions), chopped
1 fresh red chilli, seeded and thinly sliced
400g/14oz can pigeon peas
225g/8oz/generous 1 cup long grain rice
120ml/4fl oz/½ cup coconut milk
550ml/18fl oz/2½ cups chicken stock
30ml/2 tbsp demerara (raw) sugar
salt and cayenne pepper

1 Combine the ground allspice, cinnamon, dried thyme, cloves and nutmeg in a bowl. Place the chicken fillets on a plate and rub the spice mixture all over them. Set aside for 30 minutes.

2 Heat 15ml/1 tbsp of the oil with the butter in a pan. Fry the onion and garlic until soft and beginning to brown. Add the carrot, celery, spring onions and chilli. Sauté for a few minutes. Stir in the pigeon peas, rice, coconut milk and stock. Season with salt and cayenne pepper. Bring to simmering point, cover and cook over a low heat for about 25 minutes.

3 About 10 minutes before the rice mixture is cooked, heat the remaining oil in a heavy frying pan, add the demerara sugar and cook, without stirring, until it begins to caramelize. Add the chicken. Cook for 8–10 minutes until it is browned, glazed and cooked through. Transfer the chicken to a board and slice thickly. Serve the pigeon pea rice in individual bowls with the chicken on top.

Chicken & Bean Risotto

Brown rice, red kidney beans, sweetcorn and broccoli make this a filling and nutritious meal-in-a-pot using only a small quantity of chicken.

Serves 4–6
1 onion, chopped
2 garlic cloves, crushed
1 fresh red chilli, seeded and finely chopped
175g/5oz/2½ cups mushrooms, sliced
2 celery sticks, chopped
225g/8oz/generous 1 cup long grain brown rice
450ml/¾ pint/scant 2 cups chicken stock
150ml/¼ pint/⅔ cup white wine
400g/14oz can red kidney beans
225g/8oz skinned chicken breast fillet, diced
200g/7oz can sweetcorn kernels
115g/4oz/¾ cup sultanas (golden raisins)
175g/6oz small broccoli florets
30–45ml/2–3 tbsp chopped fresh mixed herbs
salt and freshly ground black pepper

1 Put the onion, garlic, chilli, mushrooms, celery, rice, stock and wine in a pan. Cover, bring to the boil, lower the heat and simmer for 15 minutes.

2 Rinse and drain the red kidney beans. Stir the diced chicken, kidney beans, sweetcorn and sultanas into the pan. Cook for a further 20 minutes until almost all the liquid has been absorbed and the mixture is thick.

3 Cook the broccoli in a separate pan of boiling salted water for 5 minutes, then drain.

4 Stir the broccoli and chopped herbs into the risotto, season to taste and serve immediately.

> **Variation**
> *Replace the kidney beans with another type of canned beans, such as black-eyed or cannellini.*

Caribbean Peanut Chicken

Peanut butter adds a richness to this dish as well as a delicious depth of flavour all of its own.

Serves 4

4 skinless chicken breast fillets, cut into thin strips
225g/8oz/generous 1 cup white long grain rice
15g/½oz/1 tbsp butter, plus extra for greasing
30ml/2 tbsp groundnut (peanut) oil
1 onion, finely chopped
2 tomatoes, peeled, seeded and chopped
1 fresh green chilli, seeded and sliced
60ml/4 tbsp smooth peanut butter
450ml/¾ pint/scant 2 cups chicken stock
lemon juice, to taste
salt and freshly ground black pepper
lime wedges and fresh flat leaf parsley sprigs, to garnish

For the marinade

15ml/1 tbsp sunflower oil
1–2 garlic cloves, crushed
5ml/1 tsp chopped fresh thyme
25ml/5 tsp medium curry powder
juice of ½ lemon

1 To make the marinade, mix all the ingredients together in a large bowl. Stir in the chicken and cover loosely with clear film (plastic wrap). Set aside in a cool place for 2–3 hours.

2 Meanwhile, cook the rice in a large pan of lightly salted boiling water until tender. Drain well and turn into a generously buttered casserole.

3 Preheat the oven to 180°C/350°F/Gas 4. Heat 15ml/1 tbsp of the oil and the butter in a flameproof casserole, and fry the chicken pieces for 4–5 minutes until evenly browned. Add more oil if necessary.

4 Transfer the chicken to a plate. Add the onion to the flameproof casserole and fry for 5–6 minutes until lightly browned, adding more oil if necessary. Stir in the chopped tomatoes and chilli. Cook over a gentle heat for 3–4 minutes, stirring occasionally. Remove from the heat.

5 Mix the peanut butter with the chicken stock. Stir into the tomato and onion mixture, then return the chicken. Add the lemon juice and seasoning to taste, and spoon the mixture over the rice in the other casserole.

6 Cover and cook in the oven for 15–20 minutes or until piping hot. Use a large spoon to toss the rice with the chicken mixture. Serve at once, garnished with lime wedges and fresh parsley sprigs.

Cook's Tip
If the casserole is not large enough to allow you to toss the rice with the chicken mixture before serving, invert a large, deep plate over the casserole, turn both over and toss the mixture on the plate.

Joloff Chicken & Rice

A famous West African dish.

Serves 4

1kg/2¼lb chicken, cut into 4–6 pieces
2 garlic cloves, crushed
5ml/1 tsp dried thyme
30ml/2 tbsp palm or vegetable oil
400g/14oz can chopped tomatoes
15ml/1 tbsp tomato purée (paste)
1 onion, chopped
450ml/¾ pint/scant 2 cups chicken stock or water
30ml/2 tbsp dried shrimp, ground
1 fresh green chilli, seeded and finely chopped
350g/12oz/1¾ cups long grain rice

1 Rub the chicken with the garlic and thyme, and set aside. Heat the oil in a large pan until hazy and then add the chopped tomatoes, tomato purée and onion. Cook over a moderately high heat for about 15 minutes until the tomatoes are well reduced, stirring frequently.

2 Reduce the heat a little, add the chicken pieces and stir well to coat. Cook for 10 minutes, stirring constantly, then add the stock or water, the ground dried shrimp and the chilli. Bring to the boil and simmer for 5 minutes, stirring occasionally.

3 Put the rice in a separate pan. Scoop 300ml/½ pint/ 1¼ cups of the sauce into a measuring jug (cup), dilute to 450ml/¾ pint/scant 2 cups and stir into the rice. Cook, covered, until the liquid is absorbed, place a piece of foil on top of the rice, cover the pan with a lid and cook over a low heat for 20 minutes until the rice is cooked, adding more boiling water if necessary.

4 Transfer the chicken pieces to a warmed serving plate. Simmer the sauce until reduced by half. Pour the sauce over the chicken and serve with the rice.

Cajun Chicken Jambalaya

For this dish, the chicken is cooked whole and the resulting tasty stock is used to cook the rice.

Serves 4

1.2kg/2½lb chicken
600ml/1 pint/2½ cups water
1½ onions
1 bay leaf
4 black peppercorns
1 fresh parsley sprig
30ml/2 tbsp vegetable oil
2 garlic cloves, chopped
1 green (bell) pepper, seeded and chopped
1 celery stick, chopped
225g/8oz/generous 1 cup long grain rice
115g/4oz/1 cup chorizo sausage, sliced
115g/4oz/⅔ cup chopped cooked ham
400g/14oz can chopped tomatoes with herbs
2.5ml/½ tsp hot chilli powder
2.5ml/½ tsp cumin seeds
2.5ml/½ tsp ground cumin
5ml/1 tsp dried thyme
115g/4oz/1 cup cooked, peeled prawns (shrimp)
dash of Tabasco sauce
salt and freshly ground black pepper
chopped fresh parsley, to garnish
cooked green beans, to serve

1 Place the chicken in a large, flameproof casserole and add the water, the half onion, the bay leaf, peppercorns and parsley and bring to the boil. Cover and simmer gently for about 1½ hours.

2 Remove the chicken from the stock, discard the skin and bones and chop the meat. Strain the stock and leave to cool.

3 Chop the remaining onion and heat the oil in a large frying pan. Add the onion, garlic, pepper and celery. Fry for 5 minutes, then stir in the rice. Add the sausage, ham and chicken and fry for a further 2–3 minutes, stirring frequently.

4 Pour in the tomatoes and 300ml/½ pint/1¼ cups of the reserved stock. Add the chilli powder, cumin and thyme. Bring to the boil, cover and simmer for 20 minutes. Stir in the prawns and Tabasco and cook for a further 5 minutes. Adjust the seasoning. Serve hot, garnished with chopped parsley and accompanied by green beans.

Rice Layered with Chicken & Potatoes

In India, this dish is mainly prepared for important occasions. Every cook in the country has a subtle and secret variation.

Serves 4–6

1.3kg/3lb skinless chicken breast fillets, cut into large pieces
60ml/4 tbsp biryani masala paste
2 fresh green chillies, chopped
15ml/1 tbsp grated fresh root ginger
15ml/1 tbsp crushed garlic
50g/2oz/1 cup chopped fresh coriander (cilantro) leaves
6–8 fresh mint leaves, chopped
150ml/¼ pint/⅔ cup natural (plain) yogurt, beaten
30ml/2 tbsp tomato purée (paste)
4 onions, thinly sliced, deep-fried and crushed

450g/1lb/2¼ cups basmati rice
5ml/1 tsp black cumin seeds
5cm/2in cinnamon stick
4 green cardamom pods
2 black cardamom pods
vegetable oil, for shallow frying
4 large potatoes, quartered
175ml/6fl oz/¾ cup milk, mixed with 75ml/5 tbsp water
1 sachet saffron powder, mixed with 90ml/6 tbsp milk
30ml/2 tbsp ghee or unsalted (sweet) butter

For the garnish

ghee or unsalted (sweet) butter, for shallow frying
50g/2oz/½ cup cashew nuts
50g/2oz/scant ½ cup sultanas (golden raisins)
2 hard-boiled (hard-cooked) eggs, quartered
deep-fried onions

1 In a bowl, mix the chicken with the masala paste, chillies, ginger, garlic, coriander, mint, yogurt, tomato purée, onions and salt to taste. Marinate for about 2 hours. Transfer to a heavy pan and cook over a low heat for about 10 minutes. Set aside.

2 Boil a large pan of water and soak the rice with the cumin seeds, cinnamon stick and green and black cardamoms for about 5 minutes. Drain well. Some of the whole spices may be removed at this stage.

3 Heat the oil for shallow frying and fry the potatoes until they are evenly browned on all sides. Drain and set aside.

4 Place half the cooked rice on top of the chicken in the pan in an even layer. Then make an even layer of fried potatoes. Put the remaining rice on top of the potatoes and spread to make an even layer.

5 Sprinkle the milk mixed with water all over the rice. Make random holes through the rice with the handle of a spoon and pour into each a little saffron milk. Place a few knobs (pats) of ghee or butter on the surface, cover and cook over a low heat for 35–45 minutes.

6 Meanwhile, to make the garnish, heat a little ghee or butter and fry the cashew nuts and sultanas until they swell. Drain and set aside.

7 When the chicken dish is cooked, gently toss the rice, chicken and potatoes together, garnish with the nut mixture, quartered eggs and deep-fried onions and serve hot.

Spaghetti with Turkey Ragoût

This low-fat turkey pasta sauce is given a lift with the addition of cayenne pepper.

Serves 4
450g/1lb minced (ground) turkey
1 medium onion, diced
1 medium carrot, diced
1 celery stick, diced
400g/14oz can tomatoes
15ml/1 tbsp tomato
  purée (paste)
1.5ml/¼ tsp cayenne pepper
5ml/1 tsp dried oregano
2 bay leaves
225g/8oz spaghetti
salt and freshly ground
  black pepper

1 In a non-stick pan, dry-fry the turkey and onion until lightly coloured. Stir in the carrot and celery and cook, stirring constantly, for 5–8 minutes.

2 Add the tomatoes, tomato purée, cayenne, oregano, bay leaves and seasoning, and bring to the boil. Cover and simmer for 40 minutes until the turkey is tender and the sauce is reduced.

3 Meanwhile, cook the spaghetti in boiling salted water according to the packet instructions until *al dente*. Drain well.

4 Place the spaghetti in a large bowl or on individual plates and spoon the turkey ragoût over the top. Serve at once.

Cook's Tip
Always use a large pan of lightly salted boiling water for cooking pasta. Allow about 2 litres/3½ pints/8 cups of water for every 225g/8oz of pasta. Start timing it from the moment the water in the pan comes back to the boil after the pasta has been added. Cook dried pasta for 8–12 minutes and fresh pasta for 2–3 minutes, but remember that these are only guidelines. Test the pasta to see if it is done by biting a small piece between your front teeth. When it is tender but still firm to the bite, it is ready – al dente. Drain the pasta immediately and do not delay before serving or it will dry out and become sticky and inedible.

Turkey & Pasta Bake

A sauce of minced and smoked turkey is combined with cooked rigatoni and finished in the oven under a Parmesan cheese topping.

Serves 4
275g/10oz minced
  (ground) turkey
150g/5oz smoked turkey
  rashers (strips), chopped
15ml/1 tbsp paprika
1–2 garlic cloves, crushed
1 onion, finely chopped
2 carrots, diced
30ml/2 tbsp concentrated
  tomato purée (paste)
300ml/½ pint/1¼ cups
  chicken stock
225g/8oz/2 cups rigatoni
30ml/2 tbsp grated
  Parmesan cheese
salt and freshly ground
  black pepper

1 Dry-fry the turkey in a non-stick pan, breaking up any large pieces with a wooden spoon, until browned all over.

2 Add the chopped turkey rashers, paprika, garlic, onion, carrots, tomato purée, stock and seasoning. Bring to the boil, cover and simmer for 1 hour until tender.

3 Preheat the oven to 180°C/350°F/Gas 4. Cook the pasta in a large pan of lightly salted boiling water according to the packet instructions until *al dente*. Drain and mix with the turkey sauce.

4 Transfer to a shallow, ovenproof dish and sprinkle with the grated Parmesan cheese. Bake in the oven for 20–30 minutes until lightly browned. Serve hot.

Cook's Tip
Smoked turkey has a delicate, but distinctive flavour because it is smoked twice – first cold-smoked and then, briefly, hot-smoked. The flavour is then allowed to mature in cool storage. You could substitute other smoked poultry for the turkey rashers in this recipe. Smoked poussin, cured in a similar way, is delicious or you could try smoked duck for a richer flavour.

Curried Chicken Salad

The chicken is tossed in a curried yogurt dressing and served on a colourful bed of pasta and vegetables.

Serves 4

2 cooked chicken breast fillets
175g/6oz green beans
350g/12oz/3 cups multi-
   coloured penne
150ml/¼ pint/⅔ cup natural
   (plain) low-fat yogurt

5ml/1 tsp mild curry powder
1 garlic clove, crushed
1 fresh green chilli, seeded and
   finely chopped
30ml/2 tbsp chopped
   fresh coriander (cilantro)
4 firm ripe tomatoes, peeled,
   seeded and cut into strips
salt and freshly ground
   black pepper
fresh coriander (cilantro) leaves,
   to garnish

1 Remove the skin from the chicken and cut the meat into strips. Cut the beans into 2.5cm/1in lengths and cook in boiling water for 5 minutes. Drain and rinse under cold water.

2 Cook the pasta in a large pan of boiling salted water according to the packet instructions until *al dente*. Drain and rinse thoroughly.

3 Mix the yogurt, curry powder, garlic, chilli and chopped coriander together in a bowl. Stir in the chicken pieces and set aside for 30 minutes.

4 Transfer the pasta to a large glass bowl and toss with the beans and tomatoes. Spoon over the chicken and sauce. Garnish with coriander leaves and serve.

> **Cook's Tip**
> *Cover the salad with clear film (plastic wrap) and keep in the fridge until half an hour before serving. Remove from the fridge and allow the salad to come to room temperature so that the curry flavour is discernible.*

Gingered Chicken Noodles

A blend of ginger, spices and coconut milk flavours this delicious supper dish, which is made in minutes. For a real Asian touch, add a little fish sauce to taste, just before serving.

Serves 4

350g/12oz skinless chicken
   breast fillets
225g/8oz courgettes (zucchini)
275g/10oz aubergine (eggplant)
10ml/2 tsp vegetable oil
5cm/2in piece fresh root ginger,
   finely chopped

6 spring onions (scallions), sliced
10ml/2 tsp ready-made Thai
   green curry paste
400ml/14fl oz/1⅔ cups
   coconut milk
475ml/16fl oz/2 cups
   chicken stock
115g/4oz medium egg noodles
45ml/3 tbsp chopped fresh
   coriander (cilantro), plus extra
   to garnish
15ml/1 tbsp lemon juice
salt and freshly ground
   black pepper

1 Cut the chicken into bitesize pieces. Cut the courgettes in half lengthways and roughly chop them. Cut the aubergine into similar-size pieces.

2 Heat half the oil in a large, non-stick pan. Add the chicken and fry over a medium heat, stirring frequently, until golden all over. Remove from the pan using a slotted spoon and drain well on kitchen paper.

3 Add the remaining oil to the pan and cook the ginger and spring onions, stirring frequently, for 3 minutes. Add the courgettes and cook for 2–3 minutes or until they are beginning to turn golden. Stir in the curry paste and cook over a low heat for 1 minute.

4 Add the coconut milk, chicken stock, chopped aubergine and chicken pieces, and simmer for 10 minutes. Add the noodles and cook for a further 5 minutes or until the chicken is cooked and the noodles are tender. Stir in the coriander and lemon juice and adjust the seasoning to taste. Serve, garnished with more coriander.

Spicy Sichuan Noodles

Cooked noodles, chicken and roasted cashew nuts tossed in a spicy dressing and served cold.

Serves 4
350g/12oz thick noodles
175g/6oz cooked
  chicken, shredded
50g/2oz/½ cup roasted
  cashew nuts
salt

For the dressing
4 spring onions
  (scallions), chopped
30ml/2 tbsp chopped
  fresh coriander (cilantro)
2 garlic cloves, chopped
30ml/2 tbsp smooth
  peanut butter
30ml/2 tbsp sweet chilli sauce
15ml/1 tbsp soy sauce
15ml/1 tbsp sherry vinegar
15ml/1 tbsp sesame oil
30ml/2 tbsp olive oil
30ml/2 tbsp chicken stock
  or water
10 toasted Sichuan
  peppercorns, ground

1 Bring a large pan of lightly salted water to the boil. Add the noodles and cook according to the packet instructions. Drain, rinse under cold running water and drain well.

2 Meanwhile, to make the dressing, combine all the ingredients in a large bowl and whisk together well.

3 Add the noodles, shredded chicken and cashew nuts to the dressing, toss gently to coat and adjust the seasoning to taste. Serve immediately.

Variation
You could substitute cooked turkey or duck for the chicken.

Mee Krob

The basis of this dish is fried rice vermicelli: take care when frying, as it has a tendency to spit when added to hot oil.

Serves 4
120ml/4fl oz/½ cup vegetable oil
225g/8oz rice vermicelli
150g/5oz green beans, topped,
  tailed and halved lengthways
1 onion, finely chopped
2 skinless chicken breast fillets,

about 175g/6oz each, cut
  into strips
5ml/1 tsp chilli powder
225g/8oz cooked peeled
  prawns (shrimp)
45ml/3 tbsp dark soy sauce
45ml/3 tbsp white wine vinegar
30ml/2 tsp caster
  (superfine) sugar
fresh coriander (cilantro) sprigs,
  to garnish

1 Heat a wok, then add 60ml/4 tbsp of the oil. Break up the rice vermicelli into 7.5cm/3in lengths. When the oil is hot, fry the vermicelli in batches. Remove from the wok and keep warm.

2 Heat the remaining oil in the wok, then add the beans, onion and chicken, and stir-fry for 3 minutes until the chicken is cooked. Sprinkle in the chilli powder. Stir in the prawns, soy sauce, vinegar and sugar and stir-fry for 2 minutes.

3 Serve the chicken, prawns and vegetables on the vermicelli, garnished with sprigs of fresh coriander.

Variation
Usually served at celebrations, this dish often includes other ingredients. You could add 115g/4oz minced (ground) pork and 3–4 seeded and chopped dried chillies in step 2. Brown bean sauce may be substituted for the soy sauce and palm sugar for the sugar. For a more elaborate garnish, make an omelette from 2 eggs, roll it up and cut into thin slices. Shredded spring onion (scallion) and chopped fresh red chillies can also be sprinkled over the finished dish.

Chinese Chicken with Cashew Nuts

The roasted cashew nuts provide extra proteins as well as flavour to this dish.

Serves 4

4 skinless chicken breast fillets, about 175g/6oz each, cut into strips
3 garlic cloves, crushed
60ml/4 tbsp soy sauce
30ml/2 tbsp cornflour (cornstarch)
225g/8oz dried egg noodles
45ml/3 tbsp groundnut (peanut) or sunflower oil
15ml/1 tbsp sesame oil
115g/4oz/1 cup cashew nuts, roasted
6 spring onions (scallions), cut into 5cm/2in pieces and halved lengthways
spring onion (scallion) curls and a little chopped fresh red chilli, to garnish

1 Place the chicken in a bowl with the garlic, soy sauce and cornflour and mix until the chicken is well coated. Cover and chill for about 30 minutes.

2 Meanwhile, bring a large pan of water to the boil and add the egg noodles. Turn off the heat and leave to stand for 5 minutes. Drain well and reserve.

3 Heat the oils in a wok or large heavy frying pan and add the chilled chicken and marinade juices. Stir-fry over a high heat for about 3–4 minutes or until the chicken is golden brown all over.

4 Add the cashew nuts and spring onions to the pan, and stir-fry for 2–3 minutes.

5 Add the drained noodles and stir-fry for a further 2 minutes. Toss to mix thoroughly. Serve immediately, garnished with spring onion curls and sprinkled with chopped fresh red chilli.

Stir-fried Rice Noodles with Chicken & Prawns

This Thai recipe combines chicken with prawns and has the characteristic sweet, sour and salty flavours.

Serves 4

225g/8oz dried flat rice noodles
120ml/4fl oz/ ½ cup water
60ml/4 tbsp Thai fish sauce (nam pla)
15ml/1 tbsp sugar
15ml/1 tbsp fresh lime juice
5ml/1 tsp paprika
pinch of cayenne pepper
45ml/3 tbsp vegetable oil
2 garlic cloves, finely chopped
1 chicken skinless breast fillet, finely sliced
8 raw prawns (shrimp), peeled, deveined and cut in half
1 egg
50g/2oz roasted peanuts, coarsely crushed
3 spring onions (scallions), cut into short lengths
175g/6oz/ ¾ cup beansprouts
fresh coriander (cilantro) leaves and lime wedges, to garnish

1 Place the rice noodles in a large bowl, cover with warm water and soak for 30 minutes until soft. Drain well. Combine the water, fish sauce, sugar, lime juice, paprika and cayenne in a small bowl. Set aside until required.

2 Heat the oil in a wok or heavy frying pan. Add the garlic and fry for 30 seconds. Stir in the chicken and prawns, and stir-fry for 3–4 minutes until cooked.

3 Push the chicken and prawn mixture to the sides of the wok. Break the egg into the centre, then stir to break up the yolk and cook over a medium heat until lightly scrambled.

4 Add the noodles and the fish sauce mixture to the wok. Add half the crushed peanuts and cook, stirring frequently, until the noodles are soft and most of the liquid has been absorbed.

5 Add the spring onions and half of the beansprouts. Cook, stirring for 1 minute more. Spoon on to a serving platter. Sprinkle with the remaining peanuts and beansprouts. Garnish with coriander and lime wedges, and serve.

Chicken Chow Mein

Chow Mein, in which noodles are stir-fried with meat, fish, shellfish or vegetables, is arguably China's best-known noodle dish.

Serves 4
350g/12oz noodles
225g/8oz skinless chicken
    breast fillets
45ml/3 tbsp soy sauce
15ml/1 tbsp rice wine or
    dry sherry
15ml/1 tbsp dark sesame oil
60ml/4 tbsp vegetable oil
15 ml/1 tsp Chinese five-
    spice powder
2 garlic cloves, finely chopped
50g/2oz mangetouts (snow peas)
115g/4oz/ ½ cup beansprouts
50g/2oz/ ⅓ cup ham,
    finely shredded
4 spring onions (scallions),
    finely chopped
salt and freshly ground
    black pepper

1 Cook the noodles in a pan of boiling water according to the packet instructions until tender. Drain, rinse under cold water and drain well again.

2 Slice the chicken into fine shreds about 5cm/2in in length. Place in a bowl and add 10ml/2 tsp of the soy sauce, the rice wine or sherry and sesame oil.

3 Heat half the vegetable oil in a wok or large frying pan over a high heat. When it starts smoking, add the chicken mixture. Stir-fry for 2 minutes until colouring, then transfer the chicken to a plate and keep it hot.

4 Wipe the wok clean and heat the remaining oil. Stir in the five-spice powder, garlic, mangetouts, beansprouts and ham, stir-fry for another minute or so and add the noodles.

5 Continue to stir-fry until the noodles are heated through. Add the remaining soy sauce to taste and season with salt and pepper. Return the chicken and any juices to the noodle mixture, add the chopped spring onions and give the mixture a final stir. Serve immediately.

Special Chow Mein

If you cannot get lap cheong, an air-dried Chinese sausage found in Chinese supermarkets, substitute ham, chorizo or salami.

Serves 4–6
45ml/3 tbsp vegetable oil
2 garlic cloves, sliced
5ml/1 tsp chopped fresh
    root ginger
2 fresh red chillies, chopped
2 lap cheong, about 76g/3oz,
    rinsed and sliced (optional)
16 raw tiger prawns (jumbo
    shrimp), peeled but tails left
    intact and deveined
1 chicken breast fillet, thinly sliced
115g/4oz green beans
225g/8oz/1 cup beansprouts
50g/2oz/1 cup garlic chives
450g/1lb egg noodles, cooked in
    boiling water until tender
30ml/2 tbsp soy sauce
15ml/1 tbsp oyster sauce
15ml/1 tbsp sesame oil
salt and freshly ground
    black pepper
2 spring onions (scallions),
    shredded and 15ml/1 tbsp
    coriander (cilantro) leaves,
    to garnish

1 Heat 15ml/1 tbsp of the oil in a wok or large frying pan and fry the garlic, ginger and chillies. Add the lap cheong, prawns, chicken and beans. Stir-fry for about 2 minutes over a high heat or until the chicken and prawns are cooked. Transfer the mixture to a bowl and set aside.

2 Heat the remaining oil in the wok. Add the beansprouts and garlic chives. Stir-fry for 1–2 minutes. Add the noodles and toss and stir to mix. Stir in the soy sauce and oyster sauce and season with salt and pepper.

3 Return the chicken mixture to the wok. Reheat and mix well with the noodles. Stir in the sesame oil. Serve, garnished with spring onions and coriander leaves.

> **Cook's Tip**
> Garlic chives are also known as Chinese or flowering chives. They combine the flavour of both herbs.

Chicken Curry with Rice Vermicelli

Lemon grass gives this South-east Asian curry a wonderful, lemony flavour.

Serves 4
1.5kg/3½lb chicken
225g/8oz sweet potatoes
60ml/4 tbsp oil
1 onion, finely sliced
3 garlic cloves, crushed
30–45ml/2–3 tbsp Thai
   curry powder
5ml/1 tsp sugar
10ml/2 tsp Thai fish sauce
   (nam pla)
600ml/1 pint/2½ cups
   coconut milk
1 lemon grass stalk, cut in half
350g/12oz rice vermicelli, soaked
   in hot water until soft
salt

For the garnish
115g/4oz/ ½ cup beansprouts
2 spring onions (scallions), thinly
   sliced diagonally
2 fresh red chillies, seeded and
   thinly sliced
8–10 mint leaves

1 Skin the chicken and cut it into small pieces. Peel the sweet potatoes and cut them into large chunks.

2 Heat half the oil in a large, heavy pan. Add the onion and garlic, and fry until the onion softens. Add the chicken pieces and stir-fry until they change colour.

3 Stir in the curry powder. Season with salt and sugar and mix thoroughly, then add the fish sauce, coconut milk and lemon grass. Cook over a low heat for 15 minutes.

4 Meanwhile, heat the remaining oil in a large frying pan. Fry the sweet potatoes until lightly golden.

5 Using a slotted spoon, add the sweet potato pieces to the chicken. Cook for 10–15 minutes more or until both the chicken and sweet potatoes are tender.

6 Drain the rice vermicelli and cook in a pan of boiling water for 3–5 minutes. Drain well. Place in shallow serving bowls with the chicken curry. Garnish with beansprouts, spring onions, chillies and mint leaves and serve.

Stir-fried Sweet-&-sour Chicken

A quickly cooked, all-in-one stir-fry meal with a South-east Asian influence.

Serves 4
275g/10oz Chinese egg noodles
30ml/2 tbsp vegetable oil
3 spring onions
   (scallions), chopped
1 garlic clove, crushed
2.5cm/1in piece fresh root
   ginger, grated
5ml/1 tsp hot paprika
5ml/1 tsp ground coriander
3 chicken breast fillets, sliced
115g/4oz sugar snap peas,
   trimmed
115g/4oz baby sweetcorn, halved
225g/8oz/1 cup beansprouts
15ml/1 tbsp cornflour
   (cornstarch)
45ml/3 tbsp soy sauce
45ml/3 tbsp lemon juice
15ml/1 tbsp sugar
salt
45ml/3 tbsp chopped fresh
   coriander (cilantro) or spring
   onion (scallion) tops, to garnish

1 Bring a large pan of salted water to the boil. Add the noodles and cook according to the packet instructions. Drain, cover and keep warm.

2 Heat the oil in a wok or frying pan. Add the chopped spring onions and cook over a gentle heat. Mix in the garlic, ginger, paprika and ground coriander, and stir for a minute or so. Add the chicken and stir-fry for 3–4 minutes.

3 Add the peas, sweetcorn and beansprouts, cover the wok and steam briefly. Stir in the noodles.

4 Combine the cornflour, soy sauce, lemon juice and sugar in a small bowl, stirring until the sugar has dissolved. Add to the wok and simmer briefly to thicken. Serve, garnished with chopped coriander or spring onion tops.

> **Cook's Tip**
> *Large wok lids are cumbersome and can be difficult to store in a small kitchen. Consider placing a circle of greaseproof (waxed) paper against the food surface to keep juices in.*